# In the Backyard

## Relearning the Art of Aging, Dying and Making Love

### A Memoir

MIROLAND IMPRINT 13

Canadä

ONTARIO ARTS COUNCIL
CONSEIL DES ARTS DE L'ONTARIO

an Ontario government agency
un organisme du gouvernement de l'Ontario

Canada Council   Conseil des arts
for the Arts      du Canada

Guernica Editions Inc. acknowledges the support
of the Canada Council for the Arts and the Ontario Arts Council.
The Ontario Arts Council is an agency of the Government of Ontario.
We acknowledge the financial support of the Government of Canada.

# In the Backyard

## Relearning the Art of Aging, Dying and Making Love

### A Memoir

## MARY MELFI

**MiroLand**
publishers

MIROLAND (GUERNICA)
TORONTO • BUFFALO • LANCASTER (U.K.)
2018

Connie McParland, series editor
Michael Mirolla, editor
Errol F. Richardson, cover and interior book design
Rafael Chimicatti, typesetting
Guernica Editions Inc.
1569 Heritage Way, Oakville, ON L6M 2Z7
2250 Military Road, Tonawanda, N.Y. 14150-6000 U.S.A.
www.guernicaeditions.com

Distributors:
University of Toronto Press Distribution,
5201 Dufferin Street, Toronto (ON), Canada M3H 5T8
Gazelle Book Services, White Cross Mills
High Town, Lancaster LA1 4XS U.K.

First edition.
Printed in Canada.

Legal Deposit—Third Quarter
Library of Congress Catalog Card Number: 2017964714
Library and Archives Canada Cataloguing in Publication
Melfi, Mary, 1951-, author
In the backyard : relearning the art of aging, dying and making love : a
memoir / Mary Melfi. -- First edition.

(MiroLand imprint ; 13)
Issued in print and electronic formats.
ISBN 978-1-77183-236-6 (softcover).--ISBN 978-1-77183-237-3 (EPUB).--
ISBN 978-1-77183-238-0 (Kindle)

1. Melfi, Mary, 1951-. 2. Authors, Canadian (English)--20th century--
Biography. 3. Aging. 4. Death. 5. Love. 6. Autobiographies. I. Title.
II. Series: MiroLand imprint ; 13

PS8576.E46Z42 2018          C811'.54          C2018-900150-X
                                              C2018-900151-8

# High Summer

# WHAT IS THE ANSWER?

## Year One

# I

Mirrors, like monsters, come in all shapes and sizes. They sneak up on you when you least expect it and take a big bite out of your life. Monsters hide in the dark. No such luck with mirrors. You can't avoid the damn things. Nor can you avoid getting old.

Time to slay the dragon, I tell myself. I'm old enough. Fight back. Better to be predator than prey.

Growing old should come as no surprise; I have been at it for years. I should be able to turn to the mirror and greet my reflection as I would a sister. She and I go back a long way, and yet each time the two of us meet, I am taken by surprise. She is old and I am young!

Supposedly you are as young as you feel. Your body is like a pair of pants with an elastic waistband—self-adjusting. So, the older you get, the more comfortable you should feel inside your skin. To my mind that's stretching the truth.

Gaining weight, losing momentum, making New Year's Resolutions in the middle of the year, wondering who I might have been had Lady Luck favoured me and dutifully pouting, sinning, forgiving, making do, baking, returning phone calls, embracing my dear old husband and adult children, looking in on the marvellous baby blue sky and savouring a second cup of coffee in the backyard, are all part and parcel of my daily life now. Having no nine-to-five job to rush to, I can retire to the den and watch TV or daydream. I've done it all—once, twice, a hundred times. And yet I can't believe I am turning the big 50. Remembering the look on my aunt's face as she lay dying, I wonder how I can possibly court joy, chase after "*Isdom*" (I don't dare call it "*Wisdom*") and expect to succeed?

"The problem is, and get this straight, I liked being young," I tell my husband, a licensed therapist. "I liked my slim figure and golden brown hair. Back then I was optimistic and sure of myself. Grey hair, wrinkles, and self-doubts—they're all part of an elaborate hoax to cover up who I am. Really am!"

"The important thing," he says, "is to be able to joke about your age. If you can do that, count yourself lucky. Knowing how to tell a joke is more valuable than knowing how to add and subtract. (Much good math skills do when you are down in the dumps.) Jokes, tall tales, embellished truths and little white lies ('I love your tie!') go a long way in making life, and more importantly, dying bearable."

"Don't tell me I'll get used to getting old, because I won't. Don't tell me to look for the silver lining, because I have looked and have not found it. I have put on rose-coloured glasses and the world did not change colour. From grey to grey. Little white lies boost morale, inspire good feelings, but let's call a spade a spade. Aging is as unnatural as turning the other cheek when you are singled out and made fun of."

"No one expects you to like getting old. If getting old were no big deal, if the thought of dying were as appealing as drinking a cool glass of lemonade on a hot day, if mortality were a joke, would life be worth living? Make a list of things you want to do before you kick the bucket and then do them. Stay in the moment. How many clichés do you need before you get it? You got one life to live, enjoy it."

If only I could do as suggested … if only I could live it up. If only I could sing in the rain. If only I could forget my problems. If only aging would come as second nature, I might—just might—be happy. I want direction. I want to take a course, "How to Age Gracefully, 101," pass it with flying colours and be done with it. On to the next challenge! Unfortunately, you can't teach an old dog new tricks.

My husband does not agree. Picking up his wood recorder, he insists that aging is like learning to play a musical instrument. You have to learn how to do it so that it becomes second nature. All you will get from a violin or piano is noise if you don't practice.

If I want to age well (I sure do!), I should do the required exercises. I should, I suppose, turn to the mirror as would a musician turn to Mozart and Bach. (What's there not to love?) Unfortunately, I can't do it. All the mirrors I come across either snarl or bite.

7

# 2

Getting old is easy, staying young is hard work—it's a full-time occupation. I should quit while I'm ahead, or risk being told: "You're fired." No one can turn back the clock.

God must have dropped out of school (trade school!) because his most famous creation, the human body, leaves much to be desired. It doesn't stand the test of time. You can argue a craftsman would get rid of the flaws before he puts his product on the market but God (assuming there is one) is more like a top-notch artist. He doesn't care what anyone thinks. Possibly God thinks of himself as a work-in-progress. A masterpiece-in-the-making.

The problem is every time I check out the mirror I am not pleased with God's handiwork. Aging is a mistake. A recall is in order. I wish I could file a class action suit.

Built-in obsolescence has its advantages in a market economy. I shouldn't knock it. Many children are dying to be born. Still, I'm not so self-sacrificing. Every time I look down and see yet another spider vein crawling up my leg, I take God's name in vain. I break the first commandment and I am not ashamed of it.

Ideally, I should spend more time doing good works and less time looking at myself in the mirror, and then I might not only forgive God for his mistakes, but my own as well. But the fact is I'm envious of those half my age. Young women go to beauty shops; old women, to hospitals. Young women have bad hair days; old women don't have much hair to complain about. Young women pester their hairdressers to work miracles and expect them to deliver; old women demand the same from their doctors. Old women are given new hips, new hearts and, when everything else fails, a new way of thinking. (A pill does the trick!) Young women indulge in gossip; old women say nothing. They might want to say: "Why am I dying, and you're not?" but luckily their lips are sealed.

8

Dr. George Nemeth, my husband and (in)constant therapist, tells me: "Worrying about getting older will do you no good. It's best to go to a cemetery and put your problems in perspective."

If I had listened to his advice over the years I might have matured — gone from stage one: teenhood (young and stupid) to stage two: adulthood (old and wise). Instead, I managed to get stupider and stupider.

Is it just me? Or is it that in every child there is a sage, and in every old hag, a broken spirit? All I know for sure is that everyone, young or old, is a Merry-Wanna-Be. If I could turn to the mirror, without prejudice, as a child would turn to a candy shop, I might be in for a treat, but that's not about to happen. Often, when I turn to the mirror or the scale, I wonder: How can this be — I eat less and weigh more? Menstruation isn't a curse, menopause is. The scale: a bad news bible.

Gaining weight past fifty is like: a) travelling in a third world country and being pulled over for speeding (pay the bribe, or go to jail); b) having your air conditioner break down on the hottest day of the year; c) identifying with a nun who has been kicked out of the convent because of a certain sex toy found among her things; or d) all of the above?

My husband tells me: "When you get to be an old fart, it's easy to feel bad about yourself. You pass gas when you least expect it, and embarrass yourself. The best way to avoid being a public spectacle is to kick the bucket, and if you don't want to do that (not yet anyway!), you have to have a sense of humour. Or at least pretend to have one!"

I get it — life is an amusement park; its mirrors are deliberately distorted. I don't like what I see in them, but what of it? It's all in good fun. Only Superwoman can look young forever; the rest of us shrink vertically, and expand horizontally disproportionately.

A scale doesn't look like an axe, but it can cut you down to size. Then again, trees get bigger with age and are loved for it. I suppose it's because they don't have an axe to grind.

I should stop counting calories, and start counting my blessings, but do I do it?

The human body can be compared to a car. The older it gets, the less value it has. (Some investment!) Of course, if I were an optimist (as is my husband), I would decide not to make such an odious comparison. I would compare the human body to the sun. Unlike a car the sun won't run out of fuel anytime soon. Nor can your soul.

So why then do I turn to the mirror as I would turn towards a brick wall — walk in the opposite direction? I would rather put up with a skin disorder, rosacea, than have to cover up my neck with a scarf because the chick in question has turned into a big bird of sorts — from fowl to foul. Why is that young people get new clothes; old people, new ailments? Young people have no time; old people, too much? A trading post should be set up so the old and young could exchange goods and services. Thankfully, love and compassion can be bartered — at any age!

My body claims to be my friend, but it will betray me. Why do I look in the mirror and expect confirmation I am more than the sum of my parts? A magician would — a mirror is an important part of his act. A tool in mass deception. I miss my youth as a blind man misses his sight. My loss benefits no one.

"The trick to not getting old is to stop focusing on it," my husband tells me. "Focus on anything else but that. The more inward your gaze, the unhappier you'll be."

So instead of turning a blind eye to the world's problems, to stay young, I should fix them?

"You can try," he says. "Having a beer can make you feel good, but having a goal, that can work wonders."

"Don't try to convince me that getting old is some big adventure, because if you do, you'll be just as much a con-artist as someone who tries to sell me the fountain of youth."

"If you want to get old real fast (and why would you?), all you have to do is light up a cigarette, or get angry. Smoking clogs the arteries, so does anger. Both are habit-forming. If you want to stay young (and why wouldn't you?), show mercy."

If only I could love-and-obey The Good Doctor …

# 3

There are those who have the Midas touch — everything they touch turns to gold — and then there are those of us who have the Midas touch in reverse. Shit happens. (And how!) I've failed at nearly everything I tried.

The man sitting across the kitchen table from me, an accredited psychologist and husband to this ne'er-do-well, decides I have it all wrong. He tells me: "At *your* age each day that you are in good health, each day your arms or legs don't hurt, is an achievement. Each day your lungs don't have to make an effort to provide you with the most addictive substance in this solar system — air — is as good a reason as any to celebrate. To be here and knowing there's a date of execution, and to ignore the fact, well, it's an achievement."

I agree — kind of. Each year the Queen of England bestows the title of 'Lady' to high achievers; actors often head the list, graduating from plain old Janes to Lady Janes. But any woman who manages to get through fifty years on this crazy planet of ours should be addressed as "Lady." Too bad that's not about to happen.

My husband sees it another way. "You can wait a lifetime for your achievements to be recognized, and come up short or you can walk into your backyard, turn to your flowers as if they were your ladies-in-waiting and be assured you don't always have to be first to be happy. Coming in second is good enough. Even those who come third or fourth can expect to be served with a smile."

I hand my dear old husband a beer in payment for his sage advice. I should stop whining and count my blessings.

Yes, sir — anyone can feel like a lady of high rank. All you have to do is open the back door (the Arc of Triumph!) and go into the garden. Each flower bows and says: "Whatever you wish, my Lady."

If I can't turn to the mirror like a clown — put on a happy face, I can always make a bouquet and give it to someone who has succeeded at everything they tried their hand at. The secret to success is flattery.

I have the will to humility, the will to courage, the will to bear discomfort, and then I don't. The fact is I'm down on my luck. I have nothing to show for all my hard work. I wear my poverty like a pyramid. I am buried alive in it … King Tut, come rescue me. But he won't come; if I need help, I should call on the living. Nine out of ten will respond to an emotional SOS. I made that statistic up, but it sounds about right.

"If I were rich I could take my mind off my problems by going on an African safari, but I'm broke," I tell my one and only.

"You don't have to go to Africa and hunt wild beasts to feel the satisfaction of the hunt. You can go to the backyard and hunt down lily beetles. They're a menace."

That's true. One lily beetle lays thousands of eggs, and the eggs mature in less than two weeks. They strip the lilies of their leaves. You can dust the lilies with insecticides, but that's bad for the environment. The best way to get rid of the beetles is to wipe them off the plant with a soapy dish cloth.

Declaring war on lily beetles is a noble enterprise. In the backyard anyone and everyone can be a warrior princess, set to rid the world of a dreaded enemy: the bad, the ugly and the not-so-good. Still, I'm not convinced beetle hunting will help me stay centred. Mother Nature throws talents in the air—the lucky ones get a handful, and the not-so-lucky get fuck-all. Some are born into the world with the ten valued toes and fingers, and some of us are born with parts missing.

Why is it that the world is in working order and I'm not? The moon and the sun go about their business and everyone is the better for it. An ocean of well-meaning VIPs control the worker bees and businesses produce the stuff of life. Surely there is some pill I can take and then everything will be as it should be—I will manage to act like a proper executive assistant, assisting my inner self and helping her gain control. For over half a century I managed to put up with the burden of being myself. I can't do it anymore.

"Why is it that everything can be fixed and I can't be?" I ask Mr. Fix-It.

"Self-pity is an easy place to arrive at," he says. "It's right at the crossroads of self-centredness. It's much better to look outwards, to admire the universe, and learn how it works. And then, if you can, find a way you can be of use. Be of service."

Personal redemption through community service—now that's a lofty goal, one worth aspiring to, but I don't see myself achieving it. Nor do I see myself taking a road trip to self-realization. There are too many road blocks.

At twelve years old you can feign ignorance and be ignored, at twenty-four you don't have to speak up to be noticed and loved— blessed youth attracts a slew of suitors. Later on, everything hurts. You are weighed down by your emotional baggage. Like potatoes, it rots. Even when it's well-hidden, you can't get rid of the stench.

"My father never accepted me; he loved everyone, except me," I tell my in-house therapist. "Here I am half a century later and I'm still unable to handle the rejection."

"Unresolved issues from childhood are like weeds. They keep popping up, no matter how often you pull them out. You have to learn to live with them. Your life has not turned out the way you had hoped, well, what of it? You have to get rid of the self-hatred, and not because it makes you miserable, *au contraire*, self-hatred has a feel-good quality to it. It works like a mild narcotic; it slows the pace and clouds the vision. That's why you have to make a conscious decision—no more self-hatred. Go cold turkey."

If only I could. Like sending faded flowers to yourself, self-hatred makes no sense.

Why can't I love myself? Everyone tells me I look good for my age. I go to the gym and watch my weight. Still, I don't trust mirrors. Every image I see of myself creates self-doubt; anxiety. (That thing I see can't be me!)

Why can't I love myself? I suppose at my age I shouldn't be asking the question. It's puerile.

Why can't I love myself?

When a therapist fails to get results he reverts to an old stand-by—he asks another therapist to take over the case. When the back-yard fails to cheer you up, you are in deep trouble. (Sorry!)

# 4

What is possible? You can't change the day into night; you can't change your birth parents or your country of birth. Nor can you turn back the clock and un-learn the 3Rs. Schoolchildren are forced— yes, forced!—to learn to read and write and think accordingly.

Growing up, not only did my skin colour match my parents' so did my prejudices. Turning eighteen was supposed to be akin to getting my freedom papers. But look at me now, I'm in bondage again! Someone Else decides if I live or die! Freedom is *not* in the eye of the beholder. I am Destiny's child!

"If I had to kill to stay alive I would," I tell my husband and in-house therapist.

"Who wouldn't?"

"Time is highly addictive. I can't get enough of it. Each morning I look at the clock like a hungry man looks at a big round loaf of country bread. At noon I long for dusk. And at dusk I crave to feast my eyes on a glorious new sunset."

"The best way to cure an addiction to time is to give it away. Helping out in a community garden or in a nursing home can do you a world of good. You shouldn't stay indoors, safeguarding, the one thing worth killing for. If you have too much time on your hands, you can overdose and become the very thing you dread."

Yes but … My mother loved me to death. Still, her advice did more harm than good. And now here I am crazy enough to think I can make sense out of my nondescript life. Why am I bothering to have this dialogue? I'm too old to have imaginary friends and too sceptical to believe in *talk therapy*. No one knows the answers to "The Big Questions." How dare this man of mine point his finger at me like some perky fourth grade teacher intent on spreading his gospel of good cheer (like dreams come true, you just got to dream long and hard enough)! I know what's a-coming!

Here I was wondering who the fuck am I, when the real question is: Who the fuck does he think he is? A fortune-teller? An economic forecaster? The weather channel rarely gets it right, what makes him think he can predict the future? My future is behind me. Anti-aging skin creams don't work. (Proven.) Self-help books make promises they cannot keep.

I tell my husband: "To protect myself from dying, I can believe in an afterlife. But there is nothing I can do—nothing—to protect myself from getting old!"

"Are you sure? Growing old will never come as 'second nature' (happy now?), but there's no reason why it shouldn't come as 'third nature.' Aim for that, and you'll do just fine."

Third nature? I have no idea what he *be* talking about.

He explains. In the wild Mother Nature does her things *her* way; life goes on slowly but surely. That's known as 'First Nature.' Civilization began the day our animal ancestors decided they could take control of Mother Nature. Outperform her. Not only did the first *Homo sapiens* dig up roots and eat them for supper (apes did that, too), they replanted the roots and reaped the benefits of delayed gratification. Agriculture is known as 'Second Nature.' Gardening is next in line—it's known as 'Third Nature.'

"There are plenty of books on the subject," he says.

"Years ago I would turn to a good book to take my mind off my problems; now 'my mind' is my problem. I can't concentrate."

"The 3Rs come in handy but not as handy as knowing how to grow your own food. If you want to age well, and you say you do, get *thee* to a garden, and let school begin."

"Trying to age gracefully is like going back to school—just because thousands graduate with honours is no guarantee I will too."

"Don't worry," he says. "Everything you need to know is learned by the age of seven. The ABCs of language, of winning and losing, of understanding (and misunderstanding) the Ten Commandments have all been dealt with before you reached the second grade. The essence of who you are and will be has been set into motion. (Sorry!)"

"Then there's no hope for me?"

"Would I be a therapist if I thought that?" he asks, certain those who are ready to throw out their preconceptions and have the courage to make changes can re-set their thinking processes and do good.

I agree with him—picking up a pitchfork and planting tomatoes can be as instrumental in self-knowledge as picking up a book. Actually, for those of us who can't concentrate (depression or anxiety can do that), gardening is the better choice. Still, the question isn't whether gardening is good for you (it obviously is), but whether or not you have the ability to change how you view the world and those in it (including yourself).

Don't I know it? I should go to the backyard and take in Mother Nature's lessons. Her school is open day and night. I'll be offered thousands of tips on how to grow old gracefully; too bad they're in a language I don't understand.

Every garden is a replica of Adam and Eve's—in it there's God vying for attention and there's a snake out to get you. Snakes age beautifully; they shed their skins and get themselves a facelift, once a year, free of charge. Each time I look at my reflection I wonder whether or not I wouldn't have been better off as a snake. They don't worry about anything.

"Turn to the mirror carrying a grudge and it will appear cracked," someone tells me. (And it can't be Mr. Fix-It; he's mowing the lawn.)

I want to climb out of my body. My body is not my home. (No way, baby!) I don't recognize myself. Give me a road map to my interior. My face is not it. What does my nose say about the location of my soul? Or my eyes for that matter? The darkness dazzles me.

Is God tending an invisible garden? Pity only the dead get to see it.

Perhaps if I turn to the mirror as if it were a door to another dimension, I might, just might, greet the morning with a song in my heart.

Someone tells me (can it be God?): "Turn away from the mirror. Fix your gaze on some far distant galaxy (or a star), and you'll be filled with awe."

Summer Holidays

# WHAT IS THE QUESTION?

Year One

# 5

At daybreak I rush out of my house and meticulously examine the garden for new growth. Like a farmer dashing off to her chicken coop, I count what there is and am pleased with the goodies God, the ultimate Mother Hen, has delivered to my doorstep. I am definitely more than the sum of my parts. In a garden the older you are the harder it is to come up empty-handed; even if you put all your eggs in one basket (your looks), you still have what it takes. (The container: your consciousness.) Hands, feet and torso are nice enough, but when they're beautifully combined and in working order, the universe has a perfect scent. The scent of a rose, or of a violet or of a smile. Everything is possible (or should be).

It feels so good to be out in the open. Unlike tiresome indoor man-made light, outdoor light is imbued with vitamin D. Natural light is the ultimate nutrient.

Out in the back I feel like I've just been released from prison. (Not only that, but my conviction has been overturned!) Like a kid playing hooky from school, or a worker calling in sick—I'm high as a kite. I don't know what it feels like to be high on cocaine, but if it's anything like being high on flowers, it is glorious and sweet.

My in-house therapist and father to my adult children was correct—Mother Nature can cure the blues. (And how!) His suggestion to give gardening a try did me a world of good. It keeps me active. And optimistic.

Helping myself to Mother Nature's bounty, picking flowers or berries, I am oblivious to joint pain, oblivious to everything except the immediate pleasure physical work engenders. Pruning my thorny blackberry bushes, my arm gets scratched, but do I care? The pain the thorny blackberry bushes inflict is a small price to pay for being happy. I feel so happy I almost have the sense I am doing something illicit. I feel like some over-the-hill heiress running off with a man half her age. Can the man possibly love her? And the answer: "The best is yet to come!"

I love to garden when it's sunny; I love to garden when it's grey and cloudy. Actually, I even love to garden in the rain, then the ground is soft and easy to pry open. In the rain the worms come out and play and I forget my troubles. I remember making mud pies as a child and I am happy. Every gardener is a child at heart; every garden, a miracle-in-the-making.

In my backyard the flowers dress me up, the birds and the bees cheer me on. I'm old and I don't mind it. How glorious it is to be alive, to step out the door and look up. The sky is a poor (wo)man's garden. And a lazy one's too.

Olga, an old friend and avid gardener, stops by and looks around my garden. She likes what she sees, but she is concerned my bushes are overgrown and my day lilies are spreading like wildfire.

"What should I do?" I ask. "Rip some out?"

I feel like an employer who has to lay off some of his employees, or he'll have to declare bankruptcy. Does the end justify the means? Is the group more important than the individual? I never thought these questions could pop up in the backyard but they do. Decisions have to be made, and quickly.

"It's simple," Olga says. "Dig up the overgrown bulbs and give them to your friends and neighbours. I'll take a few."

Noticing the shovel by the wall, she immediately takes it, pries open the ground, and helps herself. And that gives me pleasure. A Jesus-loving therapist might even suggest the more you give away, the more God-like you become, and the more God-like you become, the safer you are from self-destruction.

Later, enjoying a cup of coffee, Olga and I spend over an hour chatting about our gardens. Years ago the two of us would talk about the men in our lives, and now not a word said about them.

What is it with middle-aged women and gardening, I wonder? Why do we love flowers so much? In our youth neither my friend nor I spent hours and hours on our knees tending to our floral treasures. Why now, and not then? Are we trying to get closer to the earth, sort of making love to it, so that when our turn comes to lie flat in the ground, we'll be nice and ready?

Thought of the day: I can turn to the mirror and get spooked, or turn to the earth and witness how much life is going on underground.

I tell Olga: "I spend more time wondering about the state of my garden than the state of my marriage."

"At daybreak I rush to the garden and check it out in my housecoat," she says, embarrassed.

"Me too," I tell her. Years ago I would never have done such a thing. Being seen in public in a housecoat spells trouble. It could easily advertise a lack of morals or a lack of character but do I care? I'm middle-aged and nuts about flowers. I think of my housecoat as armour. I'm St. Joan of Arc of the Floral Kingdom, crusading for my floral beauties. Each morning I rush to my garden and God gives me a long-distance hug.

This morning I was sure the grapevine near the fence was as good as dead, and now, at dusk, I see it is sprouting blossoms—wings! In wine, truth; in blossoms, magic. The magic of good health. The magic of self-deception. Voodoo. No one dies. (Not yet!)

I love my garden as much as I love my internal organs. Every time I read there are folk who need kidney dialysis, I remember how much I love my kidneys and my good health.

The first step towards The Good Life: gratitude.

# 6

Every stage of life has its own games. You graduate from the joys of making mud pies, to apple pies, to pie charts, to slicing up the garden into a thousand little pieces and creating wonder, floral magic.

Every time I put together a flower arrangement, it's like I am making a vow to love myself for better or for worse. (Flower power in a nutshell!) Looking for just the right flowers for the floral arrangements in my backyard is as pleasurable as going on a shopping spree. Each morning is the start of a new season; I need a whole new floral wardrobe. How lucky I am to have my very own mall close by. Shopping and hunting are one and the same. In my backyard I'm a cavewoman, a hunter-gather, looking for ways to improve my chances of survival.

Flowers prove Mother Nature is an exhibitionist at heart. A real tramp. She's dying to be looked at. I guess there is a lesson here— you do what you have to do to get attention.

I spend hours looking for just the "right" vase to display my flowers in. I feel like I am going to a big party, and I have to find just the right dress. In fact choosing a vase for my lovely flowers is as time consuming as choosing clothes for an evening out. Every time I put together a floral centrepiece, I feel I'm putting myself together for a night at the opera.

The more time I spend outdoors in my garden, the more time I spend choosing which flowers make the final cut, the less anxious I am. I cut the various flowers at an angle, add sugar and bleach to the water, as I'm supposed to, and that gives me confidence. Each bouquet of flowers is a book of good tidings. It gives testament that an Almighty Creator had a plan. If a flower can't be a random event, how can this thing called "I" be one?

Vice-presidents of international corporations spend their time arranging other people's lives with the same tenacity I do bouquets. My flowers give me a sense of power and control; they eagerly obey my directives and depend on me for their very existence.

Flowers are messengers from God. They flew out of the ground to be with me.

Every child is an earth angel. My own children flew out of nowhere and landed in my body. How and why they did, I don't know. All I do know is that they helped me get a promotion—I went from being a low-level, white collar worker to being an extraordinary Lady of Good Intentions—a blessed creature. The act of creation enhances power, never diminishes it. Every mother knows that giving birth increases her net worth. It increased mine. When I turn to the mirror I get slapped in the face; when I turn to my husband, my children and my flowers, I put a fence between me and my bad thoughts.

Fences have their uses. I often have the impulse to enter my neighbours' backyards and tend to their flowerbeds. If there weren't any fences, reminding me of what is theirs and what's mine, I might become the Mother Teresa of the floral kingdom. On the other hand, if there weren't any fences, I might help myself to my neighbours' flowers. I often find myself wishing my neighbours' pretty flowers (and their youngsters!) would follow me home; then there would be no need for me to die, I would be in heaven already!

If I had everything I wanted, I might be in a constant state of fear, worried someone was after what I had. A privacy fence says: Keep Out. A hedge says as much, but you have to read the fine print to get the message. A nice pot of flowers at the front entrance is more welcoming than a Welcome Mat that indicates that those who enter the premises should clean their shoes. (Or go home.)

I tell my husband: "There was a time I used to take strolls in wealthy neighbourhoods and marvel at the big houses. I longed to live there, but not anymore."

"Why would you want to live in a big house?" he asks. "You would have more things to clean, more taxes to pay; you would have more debts, more worries."

"Actually, I do see advantages, but I stopped longing for a big house because I know I will never be able to afford one. It was erased from my wish list. Am I not progressing, growing, you know—putting my mental health first? Becoming a sage of sorts. (It beats being a crone.)"

"It takes balls to be a sage," he says, "and if you have them, good. And if you don't, remember, to forgive is divine."

"Meaning?"

"To avoid bad thoughts, you should get at the root of the problem."

"Which is?"

"Self-reflection. Navel-gazing. Asking The Big Questions."

Meaning? I should prepare supper. His childhood friend, Dr. Frank Kunz, is dropping by and he wants his usual: paprika potatoes, the classic Hungarian dish his mother made back in Budapest.

Peeling potatoes, chopping onions, quartering tomatoes, measuring spices, I see why I should pay attention to details—it will make the difference between a good-tasting stew and a foul-tasting one, but I honestly don't see why I should stop asking The Big Questions. Like, why am I a sad little mortal preparing dinner for her husband and his friend when I could have been (should have been!) a superstar with a personal chef? And why am I the mother of two adult sons who are living in different parts of the world? Had my parents not emigrated from Italy to Canada in the 1950s I might still be living in a small town where all my relatives would be within walking distance ...

Shh ... Dr. Frank Kunz is at the door. The table is set. The food is ready. My husband pours the wine, and the dialogue, heavily flavoured with anti-communist sentiment and a dash of intellectual rhetoric, has a nice flow to it. But then the two former political refugees switch to Hungarian, and I don't understand a word ... What to do? Head for the garden—what else?

Flowers pamper a room with their presence and attest to God's topnotch decorative skills, but so does the sky. The sky also is part of God's ad campaign—heaven exists! The clouds always look so pretty. So does the moon. Maybe it's a giant flower whose roots are in the sky. Praise be to God, chief gardener. And every(wo)man's next of kin. The fairest of them all.

# 7

Most churches in Montreal are open for business only on Sundays; a garden is open all week long—it doesn't have any valuable chalices or antique candle holders, but it does contain the Holy Spirit. Every time I stop and notice how pretty a flower is, I inadvertently adore God. Thoughts don't need cushioned pews; all they need is a good-looking flower and they'll jump to the same conclusion: Holy, holy, holy is the Lord who created this stuff. In Mommy Nature's Church of Flowers you can keep your change in your pocket; this church makes no demands on its parishioners. In Mommy Nature's Church of Flowers, beauty is a priceless commodity and it's yours for the asking. A thief can't make away with your soul. God is always close by, keeping a watchful eye.

Still, every Sunday I dash off to church, and every Sunday I am disappointed God does not show up. Either He is busy planning the next Big Bang or He is puttering around in his garden. (It's hard to say.) The pastor at my church, of course, would undoubtedly argue that God is very much present at Sunday service. An omnipresent Being can't help but be accessible to anyone in need of a bit of compassion. Am I not in need of it? Oh yes … Then I should do as Jesus commanded: Love one and all, including one's enemies. A tall order. Can I do it? Befriend myself???

No one knows whether God gave birth to the universe out of a wish to love or out of a wish to be loved. Does it matter? Everyone deserves a chance to love and be loved—even dear old God. Rock stars appreciate groupies, why wouldn't God?

In my youth God was at my disposal; in my middle years God was indisposed; and now that I'm old, God is indispensable. The question is: When I die, will God greet me at the pearly gates holding a bouquet of long-stemmed roses and yell out: "Come on in"? Or will God decide I am to be disposed of? And if I am to be disposed of—where to? Is Hell a compost heap, and Earth, a recycling bin?

Each Sunday I walk into church looking for inspiration, good tidings, coping strategies on how to deal with the fact that I worked so hard to make my dreams come true, and what did I get for it? Nothing. Thousands of artists are released into the wild each year; some flap their wings and are loved. Their names are up in lights. I chirp and go unnoticed.

Flowers are lucky—they don't have to make any choices—like, what do they want to be when they grow up? I could have been a botanist, searching the world over for exotic floral specimens, but I chose to be a stay-at-home mom and a punk poet.

A rock feels no pain, but would I trade places with it? Pain and disappointment are as much a part of who we are as are petals to a flower. They add depth and colour.

Yes, but … Shh! The pastor is speaking. In his homily he says it's not possible to tolerate being alive, knowing you are going to die, and not believe in an afterlife. He says that, if you are looking for proof of life after death, dump a bucket of water on your front lawn, and out will come an army of do-gooders, little brown worms. So there—just because you don't see something, don't mean it *ain't* there.

God, like an unborn baby, doesn't show his face; God intends to surprise us at some undisclosed date. To get a chance to see God is well worth the wait. God is a beautiful idea worth dying for.

Yes but …

If God were to ask me right after I died: "So what do you have to say for yourself? What did you do with your life?"

If I answered: "I spent my days in the garden, admiring your flowers," would He open the pearly gates for me? Or would I need to give more proof that I made good use of my talents? God might not allow anyone inside heaven who did not appreciate his life on earth. Isn't that why we are all here? To be heaven-worthy? If our thoughts are stained with sadness, God might not be so keen as to wish us well.

To be crushed by a heavyweight champion is one thing, to be stepped on by God is another ...

The man at the pulpit has nothing to say on the subject. Mass has ended. Time for coffee and donuts. Even my therapist/husband, who agreed to act as my chauffeur today (an occasional treat), zeros in on the sweets.

He tells me: "Whether there is life after death has no bearing on how we should live our lives. It's our job to help each other because, when we do, everyone benefits."

"Don't you believe in an afterlife?"

"Let's just say I will be pleasantly surprised if there is one." According to The Agnostic Gospel he subscribes to anything goes.

I tell the non-believer: "Whether you think of the earth as a big school, an English garden or a magnificent spaceship, it implies that Someone is looking after it. No one else can do the job but You-Know-Who."

"Up for debate," he says.

"If life is a school very few graduate."

"If life is a school, and death is the final exam, everyone passes with flying colours. *Magna cum laude!*"

"Why does living get in the way of enlightenment? Nothing works out for me."

He tells me: "In an old Bette Davis movie the actress says: 'Nobody likes me at work. I'm not good at anything.' Her co-star replies: 'Do you like your co-workers?' And Bette Davis says: 'I hate them.' And to that reply: 'Then how can you expect them to like you? If you want them to like you, you have to like them.'"

I suppose ...

Outside the church, while my husband busies himself with finding the car (where could it be?), my niece comes up to me and compliments me on my outfit. Her daughter, a second-grader, interjects and says: "You dress young, but you are getting older."

"Everyone is getting older, including your mother," I tell her.

"My mom dresses old, but she looks young. You dress young, but you are old."

Ouch.

On Sundays I hurry to church, and then I hurry back home. I could turn to the mirror and follow the path to self-destruction, think of myself as a doll that is too raggedy to be of use, or I can spend my time playing with floral dolls.

Wrinkles and worms look a bit alike; except, worms have worth (are priceless to gardeners) but wrinkles devalue your inheritance (your body). Worms work underground, enriching the soil; wrinkles also provide nourishment—bring us closer to God.

In my garden I am sure God and I are partners in life. He is protecting my floral beauties, as I am. In my garden I am sure God is a grand Lord in a grand universe eager to give peace a chance. (And gardeners, a break.)

# 8

How much is a kiss worth?

Every night my husband and I strip down and take a bath together; going on a cruise to the French Riviera might be more adventurous than staying home and recalling the day's events a-wash in tap water, but it would not be worth more than a kiss to me. Sitting in our little bathtub, a vessel of sorts, my husband and I go where no one has gone before—sharing opinions, chastising authority figures, criticizing pop stars and politicians, listing our children's follies, denouncing our materialistic neighbours, and on occasion, we come close to solving the world's problems, dictating the terms (peace at all costs).

"How much is a kiss worth?" I ask my husband, sitting in the bathtub, his legs crossed, Buddha-like.

"You can't put a price on a kiss," he says. "If you were making an inventory of your net worth, you would include the house and the car, but a kiss is just a kiss."

"Not to me it isn't."

And then I calculate … On the average I was kissed by my dear old hubby about 10 times a day. After 26 years of being a couple, that comes to …? If one kiss is worth more than a trip to the Orient (it is to me!), what's the worth of 80,000 kisses or so?

Maybe water and food are more important in the long run than any little kiss my dear old hubby might deem to give me, and maybe world peace is better for our race than any love I may acquire in my little life; still, I want what I want, and I want to be kissed.

And I am.

If you have too much money in circulation, the dollar (the yen too) loses its value, and you would think it would be the same for kisses, but it's not. Well, it's not for me anyway. The more I am kissed the more loved I feel, and the more loved I feel, the more I suspect God exists, and well if God exists, then heaven does as well, and that's priceless!

When I am kissed I don't care about doing the dishes, or whether or not the roof needs to be repaired.

A kiss lifts the spirit. Nothing else can do it as well. A joke can lift the spirit, but does it do it as nicely?

"How many psychologists does it take to screw in a lightbulb?" I ask Dr. George Nemeth, beloved psychologist to the masses of underserved Montrealers (and to me as well, I suppose).

"How many?" he asks.

"One. But he has to want to change it."

He laughs and I laugh and wouldn't you know it? Laughter is an aphrodisiac.

"I like everything about you," he says, kissing the nape of my neck, a favourite spot.

How much is a kiss worth? As much as the Atlantic Ocean? The Library of Congress? The invention of the wheel? Even if I added all the world's treasures to my list I couldn't balance the books. The marriage of two kindred souls might not be worth a whole lot on the New York Stock Exchange but for this eternal bride (that's what my tub-mate calls me) no amount of cash can equal it.

I turn to my husband as a flower turns to the sun—naturally and with anticipation he will do me a world of good. Because of him I take pleasure in the wind, the flowers, the animals in the wild, the mystery of God, the mystery of being ordinary and liking it. Did I say, ordinary? When I am kissed I am not ordinary. When I am kissed I forget I am way past my prime. In every kiss: the fountain of youth.

"You have a perfect body," my husband tells me, and at any other time and place, I would object to his assessment. But in the bathtub a kiss is a prelude to sex. Magic acts use illusion to achieve their feats, so do those who want to have fun in the sack. If I turn to the mirror prepared to confront reality, the devil will take an interest in me. If I turn to my husband who is eager to make love, I accept an invitation to the greatest show on earth.

Every marriage needs a happily-ever-after; every comedy needs an intermission. The drinks are on the house ... The comedy of Mary and George has just begun. This is a comedy about misfits who grew fond of each other. So much so they can't stop talking and bickering and fucking and slicing up the word joy a thousand times a minute. Love and joy are cut up into mouth-watering slices of fresh fruity orgasms.

Sex and love are partners in a world-wide business enterprise, importing/exporting Peace and Good Will. A profitable venture.

How much is a kiss worth? Or for that matter—if the Milky Way Galaxy went up for sale, how much would it go for? Some questions are better not asked.

Better to kiss and be set free.

# The End of Summer

# WHAT IS IT NOW?

## Year One

# 9

How can it be?—It's August and I'm tired of the pretty flowers in my garden. Does too much beauty dull the senses? Can it evoke a kind of déjà vu sensation? (Seen that, done that!) I now understand why a man with a pretty wife would turn to another woman to make out with. Lust, like a jar of peanut butter or mayonnaise, comes with an expiry date.

Spring flowers can be compared to a swarm of teens in school uniforms; late summer flowers to middle-aged career women in Chanel suits and pearls. Come August the bloom is off the rose. Or is it? In late summer flowers are actually prettier than ever and yet they don't evoke the same rapture as they did at the beginning of the season. Back then a bunch of Shasta daisies could beam me straight up to heaven. A mock orange bush in bloom put an immediate smile on my lips. Now the garden is abloom with colour, showing off its floral plumage, and all I can think of is the extra weight round my hips. My thoughts. Even my darling double dahlias don't sweep me off my feet.

Was it Martha Stewart, the gardening guru, who said that out in the open overgrown dahlias, giant zinnias and wild asters can appear dowdy but bring them indoors and they are stars-in-the-making? Plants with long stems can be hung upside down in an airy, shady place and dried. Come November the old will be new again. There is a lesson to be learnt here and it is this—you can do nothing and stagnate, or you can make changes and thrive.

I go to my backyard like a religious person goes to confession, seeking comfort. I also go to it like a person with a headache goes to the medicine cabinet. I expect my backyard to make me feel good, and it does. Sometimes a bee intrudes on my happiness, but what of it? Bees help provide the world with an endless supply of fruits and vegetables; in return we steal their honey and tolerate their stings.

Ding dong. My son is at the garden gate. Do I stop digging and hoeing? I should but I don't.

"You spend a lot of time taking care of the garden," my son tells me, possibly a little jealous. In the past I spent a lot of time taking care of him and his brother. Back then I was the head of an important tribe. But then they grew up and I lost my position. Now that the two are living on their own, I give my all to my floral darlings. And they, in turn, protect me from bad thoughts: sadness.

"There are lots of leftovers in the freezer," I tell my son who immediately dashes off to help himself to a free lunch.

I keep on digging and hoeing. Greedy for beauty, for good smells, for spiritual guidance, for proof there is life after death and especially greedy to think of myself as a good person, I keep on taking care of my floral babies.

"Go and talk to your son," my husband, busy cutting back the bushes near our neighbour's fence, says.

I do as I'm told. As soon as I walk into the living room, my son, gorging on the twice-baked rigatoni I made the other day, turns up the volume on the TV. A prospective employer tops the list of people to bow down to and be nice to, but I can be ignored.

Flowers don't say a word and we love them. Why then do I find my adult son's silence so disturbing? You never think of mothers as being washed up; you think of movie stars as being washed up; you think of doctors who made too many wrong diagnoses as being washed up. But you don't think of mothers as ever being over the hill, and yet when your adult son doesn't have a word to say to you, it's time to face up—your career as the best-mother-ever is over.

In the backyard the only noise that offends me is the one coming from the cars on the side street, and that's man-made. My flowers have nothing to do with it, they're from a different realm, heaven maybe.

As soon as my son leaves I tell my husband: "Instead of gardening, I should get myself a job and help out the kids financially. They'll never be able to buy a house, unless we provide the down payment."

"I came to this country with nothing, and I managed," my husband tells me. "Children have to learn to fend for themselves. If they don't, you haven't been a good parent—you over-protected them."

Don't I know it? Adult children have a knack of saying: "Goodbye, Mommy," because, well, that's what they're supposed to do. But I don't like it. Flowers will not outgrow the place you put them in; well, they might take over the garden, and multiply so fast you might wish you had not planted them, but still it's you (the gardener) who decides they have to go. Children outgrow their need for their parents. Maybe that's why women of a certain age start to obsess over their gardens and ignore their sons and daughters. Children grow up, flowers don't and that's a plus—they don't change. Babies are gorgeous human flowers and make you smile, but it doesn't take long before they outgrow their floral good looks and good nature. Children, as soon as they are adults, go out into the world and find others to love. When they come home to visit they expect the same kind of love and attention as when they were young and adorable, even though their own love has diminished. If anything, they view their old parents with pity, and that hurts. There is safety in loving flowers; they can't change and become something else.

I tell my husband: "Adult children assume mothers have an endless supply of love to hand out, but they don't. To get love, you have to give love."

"It's not as simple as that. You can't force your adult children to love you, but you have no choice—you have to love them. It's their birthright. It doesn't come easy, but what does? If it were easy to learn how to behave, there would be no need for schools. Or for a police force."

Yes, yes, yes, I know I should be grateful—my two sons have done everything right—they graduated from university and are in careers they both love. I should be proud and I am, but I can't stop reminiscing. When they were little all they had to do was put on their yellow hats, take out their water pistols and shoot down the sky, and the drought would come to an end—I would be happy. Their smiles were the keys to heaven's gate. That's not so anymore.

The Gospel According to Prime Network TV has it that things can only get better, profits can only go up, and, next year is better than last year, and it *don't* matter if you'll have more grey hair than last year, you'll manage to look younger and be more fit. Just follow the Ten Commandments of Consumerism (buy, buy, buy) and you will keep up with the Joneses and be happy. (Happiness is the payoff—isn't it?) Nostalgia is a big taboo in this forward-looking country of ours. Admit to being nostalgic, and it's like you're saying things "were" better. Now, there are pills to take if you're depressed, but alas there's no pill (not yet) against nostalgia.

I want to turn back the clock. I long for the old days when my sons were very young and they went off to school; migrating, like birds, from a cold place (ignorance) to a warm place (wisdom). Back then, while my husband and children went out into the world, I was left to reign in my little house. I was Snow White. I was in charge. Now I'm just an up-and-coming-old-lady who has been given too many poisoned apples to eat.

Time is the ultimate capitalist, forever increasing the demand, and limiting the supply. Consumer beware.

I want to turn back the clock. I miss having young children in the house; I loved their enthusiasm for magic wands and wicked witches and their endless consumption of good cheer. I miss their youth, more than mine. Back then I didn't go to the backyard out of desperation, out of the need to be comforted, afraid I would be alone and unloved, if not this year, then next year—a widow and an empty-nester. There it is—the selfish need to be loved, not just this moment, but the next. Possibly I am not alone. All of us are in need of a magic wand. Does anyone ever find it? If someone does, can I borrow it?

I want to turn back the clock, but do my sons want to be kids again? It might be like asking them to give up a limb.

I don't want Snow White to turn into a crone. (Or is she one already?) Twenty years ago I would never have believed this nice lady, called Mary (me!), could ever be cruel and indifferent; be a nag when it suited her. Back then my pre-school children were showering me with love, forcing me to smile at their antics, laughing and infusing me with divine joy; back then my parents could run up the stairs, now they huff and puff. I always imagined the world I lived in would get bigger and better. I imagined having more friends, a bigger house, more money in the bank. I never imagined having less and less.

Is nostalgia a meat-eating flower? Feed it and you'll be safe?

If only I could get the keys to a fancy car and get out of this universe. I long for my old body. Over a quarter of a century ago it gave me two beautiful babies. I long for my little darlings like a woman in a wheelchair longs for her ability to walk. My little darlings have grown up, I can run a marathon and yet, I still don't have the keys to a Time Machine that would see my children jump for joy on my return home.

"Now that you don't have kids to look after, you have to do something else with your time," my husband says. "I thought you liked gardening?"

I do; well, I did. At the beginning of the season I would rush to the garden in my housecoat; I didn't care if my housecoat were wide open and my breasts exposed. Why? Because I used to think of the garden as my mother, nurturing me, giving me that lovely milk of human kindness. But now no such luck. Even in the garden I don't feel safe.

Entering this world is easy (our mothers do all the work!); leaving it is difficult. No matter what our position is in life, how much money we've accumulated, dying is the one thing we can't avoid. Or contract out. Past fifty we need a guardian angel more than loving parents; unfortunately, the older we get, the harder it is to believe there are winged creatures dying to help us out.

It doesn't matter if you're the child clinging to his mother's skirt, or if you're the mother, both are in need of protection. Nurturing and being nurtured are not opposite ends of the spectrum. The role

"Then there's no hope for me?"

"Would I be a therapist if I thought that?" he asks, certain those who are ready to throw out their preconceptions and have the courage to make changes can re-set their thinking processes and do good.

I agree with him—picking up a pitchfork and planting tomatoes can be as instrumental in self-knowledge as picking up a book. Actually, for those of us who can't concentrate (depression or anxiety can do that), gardening is the better choice. Still, the question isn't whether gardening is good for you (it obviously is), but whether or not you have the ability to change how you view the world and those in it (including yourself).

Don't I know it? I should go to the backyard and take in Mother Nature's lessons. Her school is open day and night. I'll be offered thousands of tips on how to grow old gracefully; too bad they're in a language I don't understand.

Every garden is a replica of Adam and Eve's—in it there's God vying for attention and there's a snake out to get you. Snakes age beautifully; they shed their skins and get themselves a facelift, once a year, free of charge. Each time I look at my reflection I wonder whether or not I wouldn't have been better off as a snake. They don't worry about anything.

"Turn to the mirror carrying a grudge and it will appear cracked," someone tells me. (And it can't be Mr. Fix-It; he's mowing the lawn.)

I want to climb out of my body. My body is not my home. (No way, baby!) I don't recognize myself. Give me a road map to my interior. My face is not it. What does my nose say about the location of my soul? Or my eyes for that matter? The darkness dazzles me.

Is God tending an invisible garden? Pity only the dead get to see it.

Perhaps if I turn to the mirror as if it were a door to another dimension, I might, just might, greet the morning with a song in my heart.

Someone tells me (can it be God?): "Turn away from the mirror. Fix your gaze on some far distant galaxy (or a star), and you'll be filled with awe."

reversals are happening so quickly, you could have a comedy in the works, a comedy of errors or a comedy of wonders, but often the whole thing turns tragic.

My husband, the constant therapist that he is, has other ideas. He tells me: "The arrow of time points forward. As they say—if you can't change a situation, change your attitude towards it. Lower your expectations. Compromise. You may think you long for the past, but what you are really longing for is joy. There is an overabundance of joy in the universe—wouldn't it be wonderful if you could help yourself to it?"

# 10

The sun and the moon take turns dominating the landscape; so do men and women. Couples' ritual attempts to be the leader of the pack lead to fights and more fights. Too much fighting, too much sunshine, too much of any one thing is a recipe for disaster. But what am I to do? My husband is trampling over my floral beauties, digging out dandelions (did I ask him to do it?) and seemingly indifferent to all the work I put in to produce this off-colour roadside show.

"I can't stand the damn things," he tells me, indifferent to my pleas to stop hunting down dandelions.

Making love provides a heightened sense of alertness, a sense of control and lack of control at one and the same time. So does fighting with your mate. Like applying for a promotion, there's stress, but there's also anticipation something good might come out of it. You might actually get the thing you're fighting over.

You can fight with a parking attendant and find reasons to feel good about it. You can even fight with your employer and manage to win points, but you can't put down your husband and think yourself a good person. I should take my cues from flowers—they don't nag, but here I am, doing it, and soon enough I find myself apologizing.

My husband tells me: "The right thing to do is to love your partner all the time but often it's too big a challenge; the next best thing is to be civil. A good marriage depends on your ability to be civil—to get along with someone you might sometimes not like."

"I used to think the worst part of being alone was not having someone to love but, in fact, the worst part might be not having someone to fight with."

"The bottom line," he says, "is that you can only fight with someone you're intimate with. There is an art to fighting; perfecting it will guarantee a longer marriage than figuring out the location of

40

the G spot. First: Do not fight to win (losing a fight can be conducive to a good marriage). Second: Do not hit below the belt. And third: Do not deprive your partner of self-respect."

In the ring there are rules, outside it there are too, but do he and I adhere to them?

"I would never do anything to deliberately hurt you," he says and then calls me a "Big Flower." And a gorgeous little creature.

You can't be called a "Big Flower" and "a gorgeous little creature" and itch for a fight. (Can you?)

"I'm going to Budapest in the fall," he tells me.

"You don't have the money."

"If you had a job, a real job, a paying job, I would."

"You always spend more than you earn. I'm frugal, you're not."

"I have a new book of poems coming out this fall, and I plan to be at the launch in Budapest," he says. Case closed. In his mind using credit is like gulping down a pint of ice cream—it might make you fat, and then again, it might not.

My husband and I have been married over a quarter century, and still we manage to disagree on important matters. Of course, I always imagine I'm in the right, and he's the big bad wolf. (A spendthrift and a drunk!)

"What's so fascinating about you," he says, "is that you can be so soft and nice and welcoming, and then you can be so mean."

Beautiful and mean, that's me. A beauty and a beast. In a marriage you can play many roles at one and the same time—you can be a victim and an aggressor. A winner and a loser.

When a woman gets married she is given two baskets to carry: in one are her partner's faults, in the other, his love. If his love outweighs his faults, the marriage has a chance. My marriage has a chance, not because I am so good at loving, but because my husband is very good at it.

He assures me I am the central axis of the universe, his universe, and that he feels intimate only with me, and I assure him that if he keeps digging out the dandelions the lawn will be full of holes.

# II

Every garden is a practicing therapist; every gardener, a lady in distress … Some go to AA, I go to my backyard. A host of flowers: my support group.

The backyard is kind of a fence, a fence between me and my bad thoughts. I always love my backyard, no matter what the weather and what condition it is in. Even the view of my backyard from my living room window has a healing property. Still over the years I lost my sense of self- worth.

I should turn to the mirror as a weathervane turns to the wind (what is, is) but I don't. It's not my body I hate, but what Time is doing to it. Instead of trying to keep it in mint condition, Time wants to get rid of it.

I tell my husband and therapist-on-the-cheap: "We come into this world and feel we have a right to life. The right to our bodies. As we get older, we feel even more entitled to them. (We have been in our bodies for years.) So when something hurts, we automatically wonder, why? Why must we die?"

"We don't get to have a say in the date of our birth or our death. That's true," he says. "If we could stick around as long as a mountain or a lake, what would the world be like? Pretty crowded, I guess. So, Someone Else decides—we have to die and make place for someone else. (Sorry!) Let the unborn live, and the old die."

"The problem is we get used to thinking of our lives as our own, and then old age sets in, and we realize we can ask the question: 'To be or not to be?' all we want, but we won't be the one answering it."

"It's a beautiful sunny day. Stop whining."

The sunshine should purge me of bad thoughts but does it? An optimist soaks up the delicious rays of the sun, certain of its medicinal value (vitamin D in the making); a pessimist puts on sunscreen and worries it is not enough protection against skin cancer. The sunshine should influence any die-hard sourpuss (me included!) to be optimistic, and it does—sort of.

I examine my climbing rosebush like a country doctor might examine a pregnant woman with sextuplets. There's so much life here, it worries me. The same goes for the vegetable garden. Waiting for tomatoes to mature is like waiting for a pop star to come to town. When the slugs start coming out, I worry the star's tour is cancelled. A live show is worth waiting for, but what the hell?—I can always put in the pop star's CD, open a can of tomatoes and make a good sauce. Settling for second best is not a deal breaker.

Is the soul to the body as a seed is to a plant, I wonder? And if it is, when one is six feet under, will the soul have the balls to reach out for the sun and show its true colours? All other seeds do—apple, pear, and grape. Why shouldn't the soul do likewise?

I ask my husband's opinion. "Is God a farmer? Does He harvest our spirits to sustain Himself?"

"The ultimate way of showing your love for a fruit or vegetable is to eat it. I would rather be food, than Not be. The lesson of all time: something is better than nothing!"

I can't argue with that. Each morning I go to my backyard like a hungry man goes to a soup kitchen; my backyard and its hardy plants fend off starvation. Or do they? Actually, I go to my backyard like a wealthy man goes to a soup kitchen, all too aware the need to help out is as urgent as the need to gratify hunger pangs.

"Aren't you afraid of dying?" I ask The Good Doctor.

"Scared shitless."

It's not what I want to hear.

He tells me: "Dying requires no skill at all, but few are good at it. It's best to call dying an art, and those who master it, saints."

The point being?

"No one overcomes their fear of death. It cannot be mastered. Unless you are a suicide bomber, ready for martyrdom, it's OK to be afraid."

"I don't like being afraid," I tell him.

"If I were a psychoanalyst I would try to get at the root of your fear of death by letting you talk about your childhood experiences, but psychoanalysis has not proven to be of much value. It does not reduce anxiety or depression! I recommend cognitive behaviour therapy to all my patients. That's useful."

The point being?

"As the father of cognitive behaviour therapy, Dr. Low, was fond of saying and I quote: 'Bear discomfort and gain comfort.'"

"And if I can't?"

"Try—fail, try—fail, try—succeed. Happiness is not a function of success. It's a function of how you perceive the outcome."

"The problem is I took the road less travelled, and I came to a dead end."

"Turn back and find another way out!"

"And what if there isn't one?"

"Expect the unexpected. There is always more than one solution to any given problem."

I am not satisfied.

Why is it that maple trees grow taller and prettier with age, and humans shrink? In the fall maples shed their clothes, and get a new wardrobe, but brainier creatures don't get a thing. Is it because maple trees obey on command, pleasing their Creator, and brainier creatures don't? Is there a lesson to be learnt here? Do as you are told and you will not wither and die?

The Good Doctor has other ideas. Subservience to fate is no guarantee you'll age gracefully. An old tree is more susceptible to drought and pest infestations. Defiance is the first step towards having a colourful and brilliant autumn of your life.

"This fall the maples will get a nice dye job, and what will I get? A bald spot!" I tell him.

"Wear a hat."

He plants a kiss on my forehead. And then says: "Wish me luck. I have an appointment with the doctor this afternoon—at my age you never know."

44

"You'll outlive me," I tell him.

"I want to stay alive so I can love you."

Yes, yes, yes. My partner roots me in the ground. If my partner were the bark of a tree, I would be its leaves. The same sap of life runs through our veins: tenderness. If that sounds sappy, well, I guess it is. Tenderness strengthens a relationship. It's a nutrient, as important as nitrogen is to a tree. All I have to do is take a deep breath and avail myself to it.

Fall

# WHAT IS THIS?
# A SEASON IN HELL

Year One

# 12

The doctor turns to my husband and says: "The news isn't good. The results of your biopsy indicate you have a virulent kind of prostate cancer."

This is not possible. I did not expect to walk into this urologist's office and be punched in the face.

Eating a bagel, sipping a coffee, the doctor tells my husband: "Your PSA is abnormally high, as is your Gleason Count. This indicates that your cancer has spread to other organs. You can expect to live two to three years, five at most."

This is not possible. Prostate cancer is on the average not life-threatening! One out of seven men will get the disease if they live past 80, but only one out of 26 will actually die from it. I know the statistics.

The doctor closes my husband's medical file sitting on his desk; his work is done. An oncologist will take over the case. The cancer will be treated with surgery or radiation. Whatever treatment is chosen will be palliative.

"I don't want to die," my husband tells the doctor.

"You will have to learn to accommodate to the new reality," he replies, but says nothing about how to do it. The man gets up from his chair, and escorts his patient to the door. The secretary sends in the next patient.

How is this possible? Did I spend the past few weeks anxiously awaiting the results of the biopsy the doctor had ordered? Not at all. I never imagined my husband would be told he had cancer. The event was unimagined. Unimaginable. I could imagine living in a world in which I might be deprived of food, but of love—never.

Getting a diagnosis of cancer is worse than losing your job or your house; it is worse than having to deal with the aftermaths of a hurricane or an earthquake. After a natural catastrophe there might be a power outage but you expect it to be turned back on soon enough. You don't expect things to get worse. You don't expect the water supply to be contaminated. It happens in some countries, but not in North America. Here things break down, and they get fixed.

"No doctor has the right to tell a patient his case is terminal," I tell my husband. It's offensive; downright criminal. It can create a self-fulfilling prophecy. Everyone knows (don't they?) that when a fortune teller tells a client he will die, often he does—out of fright.

The cancer patient agrees. "Any doctor who fancies he can see the future should change careers. Prognoses are based on statistics and statistics point to averages. And averages don't say anything about those who, despite the odds, live to a ripe old age."

Meaning?

His cancer isn't terminal!!!!

I expect him to quote one of Dr. Low's sayings: "Helplessness is not hopelessness." But he doesn't.

I see the future and my husband is not in it ... Wrong! Trying to imagine a world without my husband in it is like trying to imagine living without the sky. (It can't be imagined!) The sky is too dominant a presence, too big a thing to be deprived of. Trying to imagine a world without my husband in it would be like trying to adjust to seeing the world upside down—it can't be done. A world without my husband in it would be like trying to live in a weightless environment. Yes, it can be done with the proper equipment, but who in their right mind would want to live hooked up to an artificial life support system?

Just a few days ago I was worried about getting old, and now I wonder why I was? Death is the enemy; old age, a dear friend.

# 13

Taking a stroll in an autumn garden when someone you love has cancer is like taking cough medicine, when what you need is a lung transplant. I look at the flowers in my garden as I would a pretty necklace on a terminally ill person—they do nothing for me. Everything I look at is stained with sadness.

God is the ultimate Indian giver. He gives us a nice new body at birth. Then come old age, God gives notice. He wants it back. Is there a method to God's madness? Or is God just plain mad—a real psycho?

My husband coughs and I think the cancer has spread to his lungs. I cough and I don't think anything of it. Every headache my husband gets, I'm sure it's brain cancer. The slew of doctors looking after him are confident their plan of attack will prolong his life. The surgery to remove the tumour is scheduled for the end of the month.

Which is better I wonder: placing flowers on the graves of our dearly departed (part of the Catholic tradition), or placing stones (part of the Jewish tradition)? Why did I ask myself such a question? Am I already thinking of visiting my husband's grave ...? This has to stop. But I can't help it; of late Death is omnipresent—like air. Or, tap water.

I wish I could turn to my husband (and in-house therapist) to help me out, but Montreal's very own Dr. Feel Good is not feeling all that optimistic himself. And that hurts.

He tells me: "The only difference between being diagnosed with cancer and being crucified is that you can get over being crucified in a few hours; it takes months, sometimes years for cancer to do you in. Cancer is crucifixion in slow-motion."

What is he saying—like cancer is worse than being crucified? When you have cancer you keep imagining being in pain, long before you are in pain. Not only is the cancer going to hammer in the nails into the palms of your hands and tops of your feet, but so are your own thoughts. The anxiety will do you in.

I wish I could turn to baby Jesus and his blessed mother for comfort, but at heart I'm a doubting Thomas. I don't believe either of the two have the power to stop Death in its tracks. Neither are superheroes.

"What will happen when you won't be around to spoil me with love?" I ask my husband.

"You will adapt," he says. I am not so sure. You can adapt to losing your hair, your teeth, your youth (well it's not easy, but there's help out there, hairdressers, beauticians, dentists and plastic surgeons are all willing to come to your emotional rescue), but you can't adapt to being a widow. I know I will not be able to do it. I see myself jumping off a bridge. I don't know if I will do it, but I can see myself wanting to do it. I will not live without love. Half my life, the life I had before I met my husband, was lived without love, and I will not return to that state of dreariness.

When someone you love is diagnosed with a terminal illness, it feels like not only is this one person going to be wiped off the face of the earth, but an entire species is threatened with extinction.

"Why are you so certain you'll outlive me?" my husband asks.

Well, he is much older than I am ... but then, don't I know it? —Death is a shopaholic. I might be next on his Must-Have List and not my husband.

"Why are you being so pessimistic?" he asks. "You can't see the City of Ottawa or the City of Toronto from here, what makes you think you can see the future?"

Yes, but going under the knife can have dire consequences— impotence, incontinence and possibly, though unlikely, death.

"My surgeon comes highly recommended," my husband tells me. "The operation will be a success."

Yes, but his cancer is inoperable!

"Indulge in self-pity," he tells me, "and you forfeit the right to call yourself a citizen of the free world."

Meaning?

Count your blessings. And if you can't find any, look harder.

# 14

Am I wearing my sweater inside out? Do my earrings match? Maybe not. At the Montreal General Hospital, at 6 o'clock in the morning, waiting for my husband to be prepped for his prostate cancer operation, I don't care what I look like. Actually ever since my husband has been diagnosed with cancer, out went the stilettos. The cold cream. My frown lines have deepened. Cancer accelerates the aging process. (And how!) Apparently, the average age of a widow in Canada is 58 (and not 78 as I had imagined). There it is—I am already thinking of myself as a widow, rather than a wife. Are memories the building blocks that create bridges between this world and the next? Television shows contain characters whom one loves but doesn't have access to; are the dead similar? You can take pleasure in their company even if they're not in the room with you … Why am I thinking such thoughts? Stop.

The room my husband and I are in is crowded with over a dozen individuals whose hospital gowns mask their identity. They could be astronauts who walked in space, Nobel Prize winners or super models, but all that doesn't concern the team of nurses paid to care for them. What matters is when they had their last meal, their last bowel movement, and whether or not they signed the necessary forms. Compassion is not on the to-do list.

In the room I notice an old couple in their eighties, holding hands, and I feel envy. My husband and I will never be that old together. I shouldn't think it, but I do.

A Vietnamese male nurse assigned to my husband's case is strangely cheerful. He dismisses my husband's anxiety about the upcoming procedure. He hands him a pair of pink-coloured thigh-high stockings, and asks him to put them on. My husband is so spooked by the upcoming surgery he doesn't ask what the stockings are for; he just follows orders.

My husband lies on the hospital bed, a ghost of his former self. I never imagined him like this—deprived of his vigour and good looks, and his optimism. But then before 9/11 I never imagined I would turn on the news and be told war had been declared. I always imagined I would live in a world where I could ignore the evening news. (Nothing much was happening.) Sitcoms were the order of the day. Office managers and the President of the United States would continue to be the butt of jokes, satirized and made fun of.

I never imagined one day I would wake up and the world would be dead serious—the Twin Towers in New York would be up in flames. How young and naive I was! I imagined myself immune to catastrophes. Now I know better. I wish 9/11 had been part of a fictional plot, but it wasn't.

Before 9/11 I imagined Jesus Christ might come in disguise, determined to do good; I imagined Jesus Christ might come and help out Russian orphans obtain good homes or help sex workers rise up against their pimps. I imagined myself on the streets of New York, lost and hungry, in dire need of Jesus Christ's attention. But I never imagined the anti-Christ himself would one day invade the capital of the world, hijack a plane and ram it into the World Trade Centre. Nor did I ever imagine my husband as a cancer victim. Didn't I know cancer killed tens of thousands of North Americans a year? I did know it, but as it did not personally affect me, I ignored the statistics. Everything has changed. Christ came and went, and now, the anti-Christ is here to stay.

The surgical team wheels my husband into his hospital room, and before the morning is out, he is wheeled out, two hours earlier than expected. Soon afterwards the surgeon barges into the room and despite my husband not being fully awake, he reveals the cold hard facts.

"The cancer has spread to other organs," he says. "I removed three infected lymph nodes, but I kept the prostate gland intact. This type of cancer is best treated with radiation and hormonal therapy."

And then he says: "Over eighty per cent of prostate cancer patients are alive after five years. You can die of something else."

"Thank you," my husband says.

Why did he thank him? The surgeon did nothing. He still has cancer.

Helping my husband take his first steps after his cancer operation, I feel like a mother with her toddler, except we are on Mount Everest. Climbing Mount Everest is child's play compared to living with cancer.

# Autumn Leaves

# WHAT IS GOING TO HAPPEN?

## Year One

# 15

Cancer has invited himself into our house and I can't get the bastard to leave. He insists on having breakfast, lunch and dinner with my husband. Even when the TV is on he talks up a storm. At night he puts a knife to my throat. Life before cancer invaded our house seems like a dream (too good to be true).

"Help me rake the leaves," my husband yells at me, annoyed, seeing me sitting on the lawn chair, crying, when I could be doing something useful.

"Don't take out your anger at me," I tell him.

"Who else could I take out my anger at?"

"It's not my fault your doctor was so pessimistic."

"What are you talking about? My doctor wasn't pessimistic. He said over eighty per cent of prostate cancer patients are alive after five years. I have a good chance of dying of something else."

"That's true, the oncologist did say that," I admit, but the urologist had a different opinion.

The memory of what that foul-mouthed, bagel-eating doctor did say makes me feel dirty. Or rather, disloyal. Like I'm the enemy. (Why do I accept the first doctor's prognosis, rather than the second one)? Cancer betrayed my husband, and now I am betraying him as well. Mortal sinner that I am! A bitch is in the making. This bitch cometh like a polar bear comes out of her hiding place in the spring, ravenous and ready to eat up whatever crosses her path. This bitch (not me, but some other lady called Despair) dances under the moonlight.

I used to be a good Mary, now I'm a bad one; I used to be soft-spoken and attentive to my husband's needs, now that Despair wrapped me up in her blanket of thorns, I'm no better than a woman willing to trade military secrets for a loaf of bread. Before cancer raped my husband, I was his bride of twenty-six years; now I'm just a lady-in-waiting, waiting for the cancer to finish its work and get the hell out of my life ...

The stench of the wet leaves all around me makes me think of that song that says: "Don't you know you're a fool? You know you never can win."

Disappointments pile up like wet autumn leaves. I had it all—a healthy husband and a promising career. I published many books—I piled them up as a miser piles up cash. Valued them and assumed everyone else would too. Pages of books are called leaves. That should be a warning to all writers. Leaves fall (they have to fall in the fall). The process is inevitable and irreversible. There are fallen women, and then there are fallen writers who are even more pitiful. The pages from their books last no longer than leaves on a tree. I shouldn't compare fallen book leaves to mangled-up bodies, though that's what I would like to do ... Novelists whose books go out of print see the characters they created lying on the ground much like generals in a world war see their soldiers, on the ground, wounded, and near death. The characters in my books were part of my unit; they were part of a living army, my army and now they're dead. It's as if my own death were multiplied. I failed the characters in my books; I couldn't keep them alive. Even my favourite, a little girl by the name of Ubu, a witch, bit the dust.

My husband doesn't quite see it this way. Mother Nature produces masterpieces galore and they're ephemeral. The joyful leafy deconstruction taking place all around us is a sight for sore eyes. Mother Nature's gallery has no entrance fee, and the art can be taken home and framed, or it can be recycled and turned into compost. (Anything goes.)

"Everything decays. That's a scientific principle," he says. "The planet, Earth, is set to self-destruct in three billion years."

"By that account, God is the ultimate suicide bomber."

"I never thought of it that way," he says, and laughs so hard he can be heard down the street. I think he wants everyone to know that here he is laughing, enjoying life, so he can't possibly die. And maybe he's right. Pessimism is a manifestation of self-hate (I have plenty of that); but optimism is a manifestation of self-love.

I accidentally overturn a large clay pot and creepy crawlers march out. Do I panic? No sir. Ever since my husband got diagnosed with terminal cancer nothing freaks me out, except losing my one true love.

# 16

My husband lovingly arranges his piles of pills on the kitchen table as if they were rare coins. In them: the stuff of dreams. A long life.

After taking his beloved life-saving Zoladex pill, my husband kisses my hands. I tell him: "It's not my hands I want kissed." And then I add: "Please stop doing the laundry. I can do that myself. It's sex I need help with."

"What's all the fuss?" he asks, indifferent to his loss of libido (a side-effect of the medication he is forced to take).

"I want to have a regular sex partner," I yell out.

"Tears are not much of an aphrodisiac."

I hit him.

"Are you going to hit my tombstone too?" he asks. And then proceeds to tell me an old Hungarian joke: "A dying man takes a cookie his wife just baked. She slaps him on the hand and says: 'Put it back; that's for the funeral.'"

Money makes the world go round, but humour does a better job of it. Too bad I lost it. I don't feel whole anymore. Ever since cancer entered our home, I feel cut up into a thousand little pieces. My wings are missing. OK, I didn't have wings, but I had the illusion my husband did. When he was healthy he flew me to any destination of my liking. He took me to New England, North Carolina, Florida, and once in a while, I managed to get a glimpse of Europe as well. Even the moon seemed close by, when he spread his wings and kissed me hard on the mouth. His kisses: my wings. Now that my husband is not in good health, he has no desire to travel or to kiss me. I had wings and now I don't.

Most men on so called "hormonal therapy" are still capable of having sex—they can have erections and a "dry" orgasm (one without semen). Most are capable, but recent studies have found that about sixty-four per cent of men lose the desire to have sex.

Why me? Why does MY husband have prostate cancer? Couldn't it have happened to someone whose spouse was indifferent to sex? Here I am a devotee of good sex, and my husband has volunteered to be chemically castrated. No one put a gun to his head but the threat of dying from cancer is just as powerful as any man-made weapon.

I miss the act of love like I would miss the beautiful city of Florence if a terrorist dropped a bomb on it. Closer to home, I miss the act of love like I miss my neighbour's cherry tree which was cut down years ago. Who would have thought one could miss a little old tree, and yet I miss it. I miss the act of love like I miss the chiming of church bells; it could be they're still being rung, but the noise of the traffic drowns them out. I miss giving pleasure to my husband. It gave me pleasure to pleasure him and now I am denied it.

"If you die before my fifty-fifth birthday, I will kill myself," I tell him.

"Does it look like I'm dying?"

No, but the urologist did say ... I can't get it out of my mind, what he did say. I miss his good health as much as I miss my youth.

The perky in-house psychologist suggests I should focus on what I have, rather than what I don't. And if I can't do that, I should recall Dr. Low's first commandment of self-help: "If you can't change a situation, change your attitude towards it."

I ask him: "If this were the last year of your life would you do anything differently? Would you retire and travel?"

"I wouldn't retire. I would keep on doing just what I am doing right now ... Believe me I will do whatever I need to do to keep you happy. I will attend to my erotic duties. I plan to live another thirty years."

This man has perfected the art of aging. I should learn from him. But all I do is cry my eyes out.

# 17

Living with cancer is like living in a house where every night someone comes and breaks your windows. You place bars on the windows, add burglar alarms, and still your house gets targeted.

Ever since cancer came and messed up my life, I find it necessary to keep my house spic and span. I must have order! If I give the windows and doors a good shine, then cancer, the thug, can't return and make a mockery of my life.

Cleaning up the house is better at removing thoughts of what cancer can do to my husband's lovely body than watching a good movie. I can't control the outcome of a Hollywood production—it's not in my hands—but I can control what my cupboards look like. I can't control how stories play out on the evening news, I can't control the weather, I can't control what my children do or say, I can't control how wrinkles keep showing up on my face but I can clean up my house. Cleaning helps me clean myself up of anger. I'm so angry that cancer came and messed up my life—angry at God, angry at doctors for their inability to undo God's mistakes and even angry at my husband for getting sick. I'm tired of the weekly radiation treatments, and the never-ending blood tests for PSA—the dreaded prostate cancer indicator. The letters PSA can be translated as SOS. Help. I'm on a storm watch. Or rather, death watch. My husband will die and then what? I will be all alone in my old age ... I clean the house and I forget all that. I, who once thrived on mess, am now all messed up if my cupboards are untidy. I must have things in their proper place. Someone should write a self-help book titled: *Cleaning as Therapy*. In each bar of soap: hope.

I rise & shine and then, bang, someone shows up and messes up my masterpiece of cleanliness.

An old friend, Gemma, an artist, waltzes into my kitchen and finds that the place is the cleanest that it has ever been.

"Things happen for a reason," she says.

"If one more person says: 'Things happen for a reason,' I will scream and yell: 'What reason could there be?—like, it's better my husband got cancer, than yours?'"

"I don't have a husband," she says, hurt.

"I could live with Stage 1 cancer, but not Stage 3. It's too hard. Either I'm crying or I'm barking at my kids. At my husband. I even lash out at my mother."

"When someone you love is suffering, you suffer," she says. "Not to suffer would be a sin."

And then takes a cigarette and lights it. I'm not too pleased about that.

Thought of the day: Smoking is bad for the lungs; anger is bad for the heart. (Stamp it out!)

Another thought: Living with cancer thrusts you back in time. Suddenly you find yourself living in a cave with no amenities, little food and no books. The cockroaches crawling about can't be gotten rid of. They're taking over the space, ready to inherit the earth. They might even evolve and turn into thinking creatures that value storytelling, compassion, kindness, integrity and the will to sacrifice themselves for those they love, but if they do, you won't be around to witness the feat. The future is behind you ...

In my dreams I am a little girl who can flap her arms and head straight to heaven, but then I wake up and see what I have become and it is not nice. Not nice at all.

# Indian Summer

# WHAT IS HAPPINESS?
# WHAT IS JOY?

## Year Two

# 18

What is happiness? If you're walking towards your oncologist's office, worried the Big Bad Wolf, cancer, will knock down your house and everyone and everything in it, happiness is finding out you're cancer-free and, if that's out of the question (your cancer is inoperable), the next best thing: Happiness is being told by your doctor: "Your cancer is in remission."

"You can continue to live indefinitely with this disease and die of old age," the oncologist tells my husband. "The radiation treatments worked. Your PSA is down to normal levels."

My husband is pleased. I am pleased. The children will be pleased. (They adore their father!) This is as good as it gets.

Yesterday, I was sure I would step out of the oncologist's office and find myself in an abandoned scrapyard, inhaling the stench of spent chemicals. But that didn't happen. Walking out of the hospital, hand in hand with my husband, I get a whiff of spruce.

How pretty, how glorious are the leaves in the fall. They leap off the maples like ballerinas from a faraway land, eager to dazzle their audiences, surprising us, amusing us, titillating us—changing colours, changing attitudes, and moods. An X-rated show wouldn't be half as awe-inspiring as this display of leafy carnage.

Watching the wind undress the maple trees of their leaves, my husband tells me: "No one can expect to live forever, but NOT knowing when you are going to die provides the illusion, you might, just might, stick around for a very, very long time. I admit I was scared and I'm still scared the cancer might come back, but I have come to terms with it. I will not allow fear to take the pleasure out of living. That would be a mistake."

Refusing to be afraid is an act of will. I can't say I can do it, still, I will give it a try ... Suddenly doing ordinary things, like stopping at a café and having a cappuccino, has an intrinsic glamour to it.

In the past I might have thought how utterly boring it was for two people to do this, but now well, there is nothing else I would rather do than be just where I am and take it all in. Having someone to make silly remarks to, having someone to laugh with you (or even at you), having someone to agree with you or to argue with you, just having someone who cares about you right in the room with you is a thousand times better than sitting alone in front of the beautiful miracle of TV and being entertained by world-class opera singers or violin virtuosos.

Am flying high, so high, I'm right up there, sitting next to God and planting a kiss on his cheek.

I would rather live in a world without electricity or running water, than one without my husband. Take him away and the world could just as well have no one in it. I am as attached to my husband as I am to the sun and the moon. Take away my husband and you could just as well take away the sun, the moon and my five senses.

# 19

Indian summer is in full swing.

A lovely hibiscus adorns my porch like a kitten, ready to spring into action and become a majestic goddess of the here and now. The almighty hibiscus can make a crazy woman sane, and a complacent one mad with joy. The five-petal wonder ought to be declared the Official Flower of the 2nd millennium, as it is truly a work of genius, at par with such natural or unnatural phenomena as the rise and set of the sun. While the comings and goings of the big fire in the sky are awe-inspiring, the appearance of an all-new hibiscus flower does more than that—it has the power to make all men and women equal under the sun, engendering a certain tranquillity and lack of artifice in its viewers. One look and you won't remember why you ever wanted to join the rat race; one more look and you will be smitten with a ridiculous love for your life—as is.

How nice it is not to want or to need, and not to be bothered by the urge to improve yourself. You can burn your How-to-Books, your Advice Columns, you can dismiss your boss's advice on what you should do to get a promotion; the hibiscus gives you permission To Be—to be nothing. You don't have to rush out and impress anyone with how nice you are, or how clever you can be. You can be a scumbag and it's OK by the hibiscus. Anyone can draw its never-ending supply of grace. Or forgiveness.

If you look long and hard enough at this incredible inhuman masterpiece, you will be grateful you are alive and inhabiting your body. It doesn't matter if you are young or old, in the prime of health or not. Sickness and death are not on the agenda when you are busy admiring a hibiscus. One blossom is enough to give you confidence—you can be cheerful, despite all the setbacks, the verbal putdowns. The hibiscus has worth, and so does everything else. A

Gentle Force rules the universe, and drives your spirit as well. The almighty hibiscus proves God is alive and well, and can do no wrong.

Admiring a hibiscus I find myself breathing a sigh of relief—all is as it should be. The more I examine it, trying to figure out why its paper-thin petals and its glorious combination of colours are so damn perfect, the less irritated I am at my shortcomings. I have the sense that I have the right to ask for a miracle, but oddly enough when I am in front of it, it is the miracle I need. I am healed of all desire to be anyone else but who I am—quite a feat for an all-time loser like myself ... Well, maybe not. As a devotee of the hibiscus, words such as *win* or *lose* don't mean a bloody thing. A flowering hibiscus cures me of self-hatred, and if it does that for me, imagine what it can do for those who don't suffer from this malignancy of the spirit. The almighty blossoms of this plant give its viewers a sneak preview of what heaven looks like, assuming there is a heaven, and if there isn't, well, the here and now is a hell of compensation, especially when looking at a flower. Any flower.

There are thousands of flowers. Some are used in herbal remedies, some in bouquets, and many others are left alone, living and dying in the very spot they came to be. In Florida, the hibiscus grows wild, but in this city, in Montreal, placing a hibiscus on your porch is akin to decorating an altar. It's an act of will.

On my porch, on my altar, the hibiscus takes its place among religious icons. It does nothing, says nothing, and yet its blossoms bloom in my thoughts. Dare I say it?—I am a different person—a better person—when I am overwhelmed—ambushed—by beauty. (Be it via the hibiscus flower or a water lily or a common rose, anything that has the stamp of the Divine uplifts the spirit and makes it easier to tolerate oneself.)

The hibiscus is my Provider. It provides me with instant pleasure. And because the plant was actually a birthday gift from my children, it reminds me of how lucky I really am. Not only do I have a good friend in my husband but I also have loving sons who understood I needed to be healed and blessed by the mighty and saintly hibiscus flower. A goddess-in-waiting.

Like a cat, grown fat with too much care, my beloved gift soaks in the sun, and yet unlike a noisy representative of the animal kingdom, the hibiscus allows me to enjoy a silent symphony. Call it musical silence, or call it a muted "I love you," by whatever name it goes, I applaud it. I celebrate its noiseless notes, and take note: I am worthy of divine love. And earthly love too. Love can be used as a microscope or a magnifying glass; it lets you ignore flaws, peccadilloes, and highlight what's truly worth looking at. The hibiscus reminds you of all these things. (How can it not?) The hibiscus and other made-in-heaven flowery artefacts help you return to a State of Innocence, meaning that you can once again love as only a child can love, unconditionally and without reservation.

I dare say: "Love me, world, and I will love you. Don't love me and the hibiscus and its floral cousins will make up for it."

# 20

Waking up my husband tells me: "You are the star of my life. A splendid sight."

Few master the art of unconditional love; my husband mastered it to a T. My husband kisses me and I can be sure of one thing—kisses are ropes tying two people together. (They're better at keeping a couple together than the fear of not having enough money to pay the bills.)

Two out of three prostate cancer victims lose their sex drive but not my husband. (Praise the Lord!) If my husband didn't take pleasure in sex, the act would be as much fun as taking your clothes off at a doctor's office and being examined for genital warts.

"Giving pleasure is an aphrodisiac," my husband tells me. "I'm so happy I can still give you an orgasm. I'm a professor, psychologist and tongue master. I feel so good."

"You sound manic."

"You would be too if your death sentence had just been commuted."

"Aren't you ever worried your cancer might come back?"

"Nobody lives forever. What kind of psychologist would I be if I didn't follow my own advice? I tell my patients to think positive. And that's what I do. I am not planning to die anytime soon. Not this week, not this month, not this year. Not yet. Those are the magic words—*not yet*."

"What if those words, *not yet*, fail to do the trick (decrease anxiety)?"

"I always tell my patients to enjoy life in a way as to enjoy the small pleasures and joys of each day, because there are always some. These little joys help us get through difficult times, and also generate in us the feeling of some pleasant and positive anticipation that there is hope. Hope is extremely important. There are still good things to come."

This is a tutorial on self-reliance, given by a man who oozes self-confidence and good humour.

"Whether you're in the prime of your life, or on your deathbed, you have a right to pleasure," he says. "You can't feel good about yourself—be happy, really happy—unless you have a role. I was lucky. As a psychologist I tried to lessen suffering. I was of use. A client the other day stopped me on the street and thanked me for supporting him through a difficult time. I was so touched. I did good."

"You did. You did a fine job of loving me."

He tells me: "I noticed in the sayings of Jesus Christ that he was a good psychotherapist and counsellor and many of the passages that one can read in the gospel refer to suggestions on how to lead a worthwhile and good life. Of course, there were other therapists in the great human culture; the Buddha was one of them. I think we ought to have some more, and particularly those who can interpret properly the teachings of these individuals, not just in words but in deeds as well."

"Are you one?"

"I am just an old man who wants to live long and prosper. This year I know what it means to be happy. Your presence, that's all I need."

Being needed is more pleasurable than taking a dip in the ocean or in an Olympic diving pool; why, it's even better than being kissed, and that's very pleasurable. Eating, drinking and fucking are all wonderful corporal delights, but what really ranks as Number One is being ranked as someone's Number One.

"Thank you," I say.

"Why thank me?"

"You kept me sane."

"You underestimate yourself. You don't know how lovely you are."

Later, when he goes downstairs, and I am upstairs, he calls out: "Where is my beautiful?" And then: "Where is my beautiful, beautiful beauty?"

A camel can store water in its hump for up to three months; I wish I could store my husband's love in some kind of spirit hump and be able to travel from here to God knows where on my own, but I can't. I need him right where he is—here with me, loving me, in order for me to get through any one given day.

I am as dependent on my husband's love as are plants on the rain and the sun. Plants don't need to be admired, but I need my husband's admiration before I can show off my pretty thought-petals. Plants aren't diminished if someone doesn't admire or love them. Weeds are not loved at all, and they are the ones that flourish. Possibly the less you depend on love the more you will thrive, but what of it? I prefer to be a rare orchid, hidden from view.

Like a pilot is dependent on her plane, like her passengers are dependent on her navigational skill, I am dependent on my husband. Call a pilot a drunk and she is out of a job. Call me a widow and what am I? Half-dead—that's what I would be. Someone might go around looking like me, laughing like me, thinking like me, but it won't be me. Lazarus was dependent on Jesus' love to be returned to the land of the living. My husband's love almost does as much, providing me with quick access to Divine Grace.

As ivy clings to a wall and flowers to their stems, as fish cling to water and worms to earth, as stars cling to the night sky, and as a drowning victim mercilessly clings to her rescuer, I cling to my husband and I am surprisingly happy.

The world needs its oceans to be clean, and its fish, healthy. It needs the moon to sit in the sky and give light. If the moon were blown up, ecological disasters would ensue. So too would I be a mess without my husband's love.

Now I don't know how to end this Declaration of Dependency. A confirmed bachelor or bachelorette might frown at my dependency, thinking it as bad as an addiction to crack cocaine, but they don't need to be taken care of. I do.

"Mary, don't be afraid," he says. "I will love you forever and a day."

Every "I love you" is a gift; every gift: unearned grace. Every flower: a snapshot of God. Every bridal bouquet: proof the best is yet to come.

71

# 21

Planting spring bulbs in the autumn requires a leap of faith—you have to be confident the bulbs will survive the winter; they won't rot or be eaten by ever-hungry, bushy-tailed critters.

Thought of the day: Optimism is part and parcel of our DNA. It's part of our survival mode.

Planting spring bulbs is a good form of exercise. Often you go to a gym because you are not satisfied with your body, but in a garden, like in a pastry shop, you are generally satisfied with what you have. Planting spring bulbs combines the benefits of going to the gym and a trip to a pastry shop. There is an important lesson to be learned here and it's this: Gratitude is the antidote to fighting aging or whatever it is that ails you.

Planting spring bulbs is akin to family planning—you have to plant the bulbs at the optimum time. (Certainly before the frost sets in.) The earlier they're planted, the earlier they'll flower. Also, the bulbs have to be placed at least six inches deep; this way they'll be less likely to be eaten by squirrels. Squirrels stock up for the winter, shoplifting at the local supermarkets—our backyards. Actually tulip bulbs are quite edible—they can be fried and eaten like onions, but unless there's a war or famine, most of us won't find them all that appetizing. Squirrels on the other hand can't wait to get their tiny paws on them. Luckily, they don't like narcissus bulbs; planting them alongside the tulip bulbs will protect them from the predators.

The bulbs need to be planted in groups, or they'll go unnoticed. There is a lesson here—there is strength in numbers. That's why men and women join together in holy matrimony, have families, form alliances ...

Gardening provides a quick fix. It removes anxiety, replacing bad thoughts with good ones. In the 17th century tulip bulbs were worth their weight in gold (literally) but nowadays you can buy them for a few pennies. You don't have to be rich to arm yourself.

Is God inside the bulbs, I wonder? Or is God hiding inside the worms. If I slice one up, will God cry, Ouch? Or is God more like air—indifferent to pain? He gives life, but He himself is not alive. Well, God was alive but after He gave birth to the universe, He died, exhausted but happy, knowing his offspring could manage without Him. In God's eyes no one needs to be cured of cancer, because dying is the ultimate achievement. In dying, everyone becomes one with Him.

Another thought of the day: There is no point playing the game of hide and seek with God. He will never be found. It's better to keep on planting bulbs and concentrate on making what is not beautiful, beautiful—if not this year, then next year.

Christmas is coming ... Once upon a time there was no space for you on earth, and then you crash landed onto this watery planet of ours and made waves. You're here for good. And if you are, then everyone else is too. Trust your instincts—no one dies. And if that's not the case, then you can always plant a sapling and hope one day to eat its fruit. In each apple, pear or peach tree: a baby messiah—the promise of a long and useful life.

Christmas is coming ... Are our bodies gift wrapping and our souls presents for the Master of the Universe? And if they are, is Death a supernatural Santa Claus ...? All we can be certain of is that the gift of life comes nicely wrapped. The moon, the stars and the sun make delightful decorations. Think outside the box.

The three leafless maples in my backyard remind me of the Magi, the three wise men; they stand about waiting for a Messiah to come into the world and make it a better place. Maple trees come bearing gifts—liquid gold, maple syrup, but I will have to wait for the spring to receive them. (Better late than never.)

Christmas is coming ... In the old port: fireworks. Out on the porch: Christmas lights galore. In each Christmas light: a Star of Bethlehem in miniature. Share the merry.

The Coldest Winter in Memory

# WHAT IS IT LIKE TO DIE?

Year Nine

# 22

Suddenly there are too many hours in a day—too many hours to grieve. My husband is dead and I can't stop crying. I find myself crying on the bus, at the supermarket, in a movie theatre, in a restaurant, anywhere and everywhere, any time. I know I should be crying at home, out of sight, but I can't help myself. It's as if my body were a vessel, and all that it contains is salty tears. Nothing else can come forth from this lady, but grief. My husband's death broke me.

A morning hour is the same as an evening hour. I have no structure. No time frame. I am worse than a broken clock, because there is no one living in this part of the galaxy that can fix me. When my husband was alive and I was all broken up inside, my husband could get me up and working again—not all the time, but most of the time. But now that he's dead (there I said it again: my husband is dead!) I'm done for.

Relief from loneliness is possible. Animals are good at helping humans deal with loneliness. But the grief of a widow is so fierce that no dog or cat can help. Even good friends can't help a grieving widow feel less alone.

When you are grieving it's like living next to a man who you suspected is a terrorist, and now there is evidence that he is. More than personal safety is at issue—an entire city (your soul) is at risk of being blown up.

Sometimes, a day goes by and my grief is nicely stored in an airtight container, and then the night comes, and the container pops open. The noxious fumes come out and I can't breathe.

The only time I don't feel alone is when I imagine my late husband is in the room with me. Why shouldn't he be here with me? The soul lives on. That's what the Catholic Church tells us, isn't it?

If he were here, would he tell me that a trip to the zoo is good for the morale but not half as good as a trip down memory lane? If he were here would he encourage me to recall all the beautiful things he used to say to me (I wrote them down when he was still around precisely so I would not forget!): "You are the star of my life, a splendid sight, my sweet Mary, my good Mary, my big flower." On occasion he would call me "The Mountain Flower of the Abruzzi," and when I was angry, "The Menacing Mountain Flower of the Abruzzi." When we would go shopping, and he would lose sight of me, he would inevitably shout at the top of his lungs: "Where is my beautiful, beautiful beauty?" And then Miss Ugly Duckling would show up; well, those around would be in for quite a surprise. Of course, I inevitably accused him of being blind and demented, but he kept complimenting me anyway, fool that he was. And now I miss that old fool. How I miss him.

I dread the future. Never to delight in a shared joke. Never to enter the communion of couples and see the world as a unit. Never to break the silence with inanities and think it a feat. Never to fix a meal for a man and be thought the best chef in the world.

There it is—never to wake up next to my husband and be desired by him. Never to linger in bed and take pleasure in watching a good show on TV. Never to hear him calling my name in his accented English. Never to share a cup of coffee together. (My husband loved his morning coffee like an Olympic champion loves his medals.) Never to …

A voice in my head tells me (is it my late husband?): "This 'Never-To-Do' list is never-ending. A 'To Do' list is shorter and it's more useful. In other words, concentrate on what you can do, rather than on what you can't do."

If only I could make a bucket list, and do the things on it. But I'm in the dark. Grief is a blindfold. I am either taking the wrong bus, or I am getting off at the wrong bus stop. I'm always finding myself lost, and not where I should be: at home with my husband.

For this widow crying in public is as easy to do as pushing a button in an elevator. Up, down ... down to a bottomless pit.

Crying in public is as welcome as a smelly fart. At least, one can laugh away a fart, but what does one do with a weeping widow? Strangers are not about to put their arms round her, and actually if they would, the last thing a widow would want is to have strangers stop and stare, let alone burden her with their concern.

Crying in public is as unwelcome as are dandelions in a front yard. I won't say crying is like ragweed. It's against the law to have ragweed growing in your yard, but it's not against the law to cry in public. If you lived in a totalitarian state, it might be dangerous, you might be picked up ... It's good that North America has its autocrats in check, or they might do the unthinkable—make unhappiness a crime. OK, tears are not a banned substance; still they are an irritant and most people do not like them. Who wants to hear someone they don't know cry their heart out? It's worse than having to put up with someone who picks up a guitar or trumpet and has no idea how to play it.

I find myself crying on my way to the pharmacy, where I would like to buy pills to stay sane, but all it has is Aspirin and Tylenol and they will not take away the insanity of grief.

I find myself crying on my bed because I lack the sexual ease of someone who is calmly and gently brought to orgasm by one's dear old husband. (Mine did it all the time.).

At night, I get into bed and watch TV, just like I did when my husband was alive, but then, it was fun, and now it isn't. His enthusiasm for what he was watching enthused me. Now all I see on TV are young couples kissing, and falling in love. They're at the crossroads of a new and wonderful adventure, and widows, like me, are at the end of it. The clock can't be turned back. Like trying to unfire a gun that has been fired. Can't get that bullet back into the gun. The same goes for tears.

Tears come as naturally as sound comes out of a radio. That's not it—there is nothing natural about the sound that comes out of a radio. It needs electricity or batteries. But it doesn't take much for tears to come out.

The song, "Cry me a river," could be an anthem for widows. This river, made of tears, might be the very one which individuals cross on a barge when they travel from this world to the next. If it weren't for this river of tears, they might not be able to get to the Other Side. This would give a purpose to a widow's tears. If my husband (and in-house therapist) were around, he might say something like: "Go ahead, cry as much as you like. It will do you good. Alcohol is used to sanitize wounds; tears do as much. Don't be afraid—you'll get through this."

A child's smile is like a machine gun. It can gun down despair. So can the love of a good man. I had it and now I don't.

# 23

The night sky is in need of stars. My house is in need of my late husband. My house misses him as much as I do. The moment he died the house noted his absence. At first it was just the walls that cried. (But that could have been the humidity.) Then the windows demanded to be cleaned. When my husband didn't come to clean them, the windows refused to cheer me up. And because he didn't return to plaster my body with kisses, the cracks in the foundation get bigger and bigger. Down came my house. Death: an earthquake with an 8.6 magnitude. It has enough force to destroy an entire city.

A wrecking ball can topple a house, but so can the death of its owner. You need a permit to topple a house, but there are no laws to protect those you love from dying. You can insist your husband is more valuable than a 19th century cathedral, and still cancer will come with its demolition team. Cancer reduced my husband to rubble, and now my house is not safe. I cleaned the windows, changed the doors, re-enforced the foundation, but still, it's not a good place to live.

My house misses my husband like a horse misses his master when it is sold off and sent to the slaughterhouse, sensing things are going from bad to worse. Nothing stays the same forever. That's a fact.

My house misses my husband like a boy lost in the woods misses his bedroom, or like a runaway misses her family after she finds out grownups are babies in disguise. (They're monsters too, but that's another story.) If children would only obey their parents they might not get into trouble, but what does that matter when they're lost? I'm lost.

The ads on TV say there are places to discover, but the only place I want to visit is my very own house, the one that had my late husband in it. When he was around, he singled me out as a Vestal Virgin, and where I stood was a temple. Now, it's just a sad little house with one person in it.

You can argue that a house cannot miss anything. A house can be sold and that's the end of it. Unless it's a heritage site, there are no laws to protect it from demolition. (There aren't any for mine.) But the fact is my husband and I were married in the Catholic Church; it insists Jesus brings the dead to life. The question is: Can Jesus resurrect my husband—if not in this planetary system, perhaps in another one?

The night sky is in need of stars. My house is missing my late husband like sailors would miss the North Star if suddenly the constellations got moved around. But they won't be. They've been in the same place for thousands of years. So why shouldn't it be the same for people? Are we not better than stars? We can think, build rockets to get to the moon, and still the stars outlive us. (How unfair is that!)

My house misses my husband like a crib misses a baby when the wished-for-baby doesn't show up. It's not the crib that is doing the missing, but the parents. They're crying their eyes out. Still, babies are born every day and some are unwanted; it's possible one of them will find his way into the childless couple's dream home. But I know my husband won't come back home—ever! That's the difference.

My house is missing my husband like the world would miss art, if artists went on strike and decided it wasn't worth the effort to create what may go unnoticed. My house is missing my husband like my body would miss its intelligence if I suddenly lost all my marbles. Actually, I may have lost them when I lost my husband's *joie de vivre*. I used to be mistress of this house; now I live in it like a church mouse—uninvited, unwanted, and unessential.

What would my husband, the late Dr. George Nemeth, a practicing psychologist, say to all this? Would he remind me that once upon a time I wasn't all that fond of our house? I often complained it wasn't big enough for a family of four. (It wasn't.) Well, knowing him, and his penchant for wanting to make others feel good, he might not remind me of my follies. He might tell me: "A house contributes to your net worth, but you have more than a roof over your head. You have two adult sons. Treasure them."

A house full of children inspires good feelings. Even when the children are all grown up, if they are yours, they inevitably provide comfort. But that's not the case for me anymore. The knowledge that my children are suffering the lack of a father makes my plight worse.

One year, as a Father's Day gift, my sons spelled out the top 10 reasons why they thought he was the best father in the world and they included: a) He supported them in everything they chose to pursue; b) He helped them through difficult times in their lives; c) His expectations of them were reasonable—they didn't have to be first, though they ought not to be last; d) He showed them how to enjoy life, setting an example for them with his sense of humour and laughter, and inspiring them with his courage and independence, and e) He taught them to devote their lives as much to helping others as to making a living.

There is no respite from grief. My sons and I are missing the head of our household like the world would miss its history if suddenly there were a nuclear explosion and all its archives would be lost. Everything is gone. There is no way one can get used to this.

How is it possible my husband is dead, and I am not? How is it possible, one person dies, and another is born? Is the womb a recycling bin?

I would like to ask my husband: "Is it true no one dies, everyone is reborn?" But how can I ask him? I can't.

That voice in my head tells me to go out to the backyard and take in the night sky and be amazed.

I am amazed. The night sky is pretty, but what of it? I still miss my husband as a ship's captain would miss his satellite connection to the national coast guard if it suddenly broke down. SOS. I can't find my way home.

That voice in my head tells me: "Even after stars have died, their light reaches us. No matter how far away they are, they can still be of help. Those who pass from one world to the next can also provide light. And direction. You don't have to be close to the stars, or know their names, to take in the warmth of their embrace. So it is with those who have died."

All very well, but my dear husband if he were around would counsel me to keep company with the living, and not with the dead.

Insists that voice in my head: "The universe is your house. It's ever-present. No one dies. In the human DNA: the God particle—love everlasting."

Now I'm sure of it—that voice in my head cannot belong to my husband. That man was an agnostic. He wouldn't ask his patients to lean on God when they were in need of assistance. He would ask them to find someone more substantial, someone closer to home. An individual had to feel good, because that was the proper way of being. (To feel good!) Anything else was unacceptable.

That voice in my head can't be the real deal—it can't be my late husband. (Dr. Feel Good!) It has no authority to speak in his name.

I need something more tangible than the night sky to cheer me up. I need my husband. Where is he? He's not in the kitchen making supper, or in the living room, watching *Star Trek*. He's gone for good.

I miss him as much as a girl would miss her freedom if an old fat guy married her, and then locked her up, afraid of losing the one thing he values more than his wealth. That girl can never go home again, nor can I. I miss my husband like my eyes miss the light when it is dark.

Lose someone you love and you don't have to ask the question: "What is it like to die?" You already know the answer.

# 24

Insomnia hits. I have lost my ability to sleep. When my late husband lay next to me in my bed I had no problems falling asleep. He was my sleeping aid.

Often I find myself calling out to my late husband: "Help me sleep." It's more like a prayer than an emotional SOS. Here I am praying to my late husband like farmers during a rainstorm pray to their patron saint for the sun to return and bless their crops. I want the rain of bad thoughts to stop, but it doesn't.

Political prisoners are often tortured by not being allowed to sleep. Sometimes I wonder if I am being punished for not loving my husband enough. A stupid thought, but there it is. A perfect wife would have overlooked the complications cancer inflicted but I couldn't wait for the whole thing to be over and done with. Insomnia is my punishment for not being the perfect wife.

At night, in my bed, all I hear is the exaggerated ticking of a clock ... I suspect a man with a knife will come round and cut this little girl's throat. A psychopathic killer is on the loose and he knows a husband is not sharing my bed. I'm an easy target. Maybe an angel will take pity and fix my wings (my thoughts). I can't.

Someone knocks on my skull. (Can it be my late husband and beloved therapist of sorts?): "First you expected your husband to be a knight in shining armour (he wasn't), and now that you don't have a husband, you expect an angel to fix whatever it is that's ailing you. Get off your high horse, and do something. Be of use. Be of service."

How can I be of use? My children are grown up. They are busy being young men, building careers, loving their partners, seeing the world. They're far, far away. They don't need me.

The only person in this little galaxy of ours who needed me, and did not punish me for being imperfect is now dead. No wonder I can't sleep. There is no one to love me.

# 25

Despair follows me everywhere I go; it has an awful stench. The thought of suicide surfaces. After my husband died, the situation was so new, there was a certain excitement to it, but now that's over. For a while I foolishly believed my husband would visit me; I expected he would come and show off his new spirit form, and assure me: "No one dies." His visit would generate extreme pleasure. It's only starting to dawn on me that my husband is not coming back and that I will be alone, not for just one day, but for the rest of my life.

The idea of killing myself provides relief. Like imagining myself by the sea and walking along the beach, I think of suicide as a holiday—a holiday from pain. Suicide, like going parasailing for the first time, has something adventurous about it. For those who are not depressed, it sounds stupid to compare suicide to parasailing, but, for those who are, the thought of suicide feels comforting— freedom at last!

I don't expect suicide to put an end to my existence; I simply expect it to put an end to my unhappiness. I am important to the world of myself. I can't wait to become the real me—happy and useful. It's as if my body were a musical instrument, and suicide the virtuoso that will play it, and give it value.

I don't want to be a widow anymore. Being "the surviving partner" is like surviving a flood with your house intact, while everyone else's house was swept away. Your neighbours have nothing, so you can't feel good. Or you can compare being the surviving partner to having a rose garden that has won prizes in your neighbourhood— deemed the best on the block—and then suddenly the genetically-modified roses attract pests, creating havoc in your area, and it's your fault. You go from being the most loved gardener in your neighbourhood to being the most despised! Actually, it's a lot worse than that. It's like being in a car accident—a little girl was hit and you did it. You killed her. You would exchange places with that little girl but you can't do it.

The problem is, suicides tell God that He is unlovable and his universe was a big mistake. That might not sit well with a Supreme Being … I don't care. I don't want to be a widow anymore. When my husband was part of my life, I had an obligation to stay alive, but now I don't. I take the phone off the hook and wonder: "Is today a good day to die?"

Like getting undressed on a hot day, I want to get rid of my body, it's too heavy.

That voice in my head (is it my late husband?) tells me: "Suicide is not a viable alternative."

Yes, sir—there are better things to do than count the ways to do yourself in. There are movies to see, recipes to try out, and lovely places to visit, but what of it? It's the past I want, not the future.

That voice in my head tells me: "You're one lucky broad. You have a Time Machine. Use it."

What he *be* talking about? A Time Machine? That's a laugh.

All I see is waste. Too much stuff, too many people. It's time to make my exit … STOP!

On the kitchen counter, next to the block of knives, are my husband's love letters.

I immerse myself in their contents, and soon enough I am travelling back in time … Born-again Christians have to go to Jerusalem to retrace the steps of Jesus Christ to drink of the Holy Grail, but I don't have to go that far. I simply have to drink in the contents of the love letters and am nourished. What was, is.

# LOVE LETTERS TO MY WIFE

**February 14<sup>th</sup>**

*My most precious Mary,*
I'll soon be 41 years old and this is my first love letter I ever actually
sent. (I wrote a few a long time ago, but always tore them up.) I was
tempted to imitate your own style, turbulent, overheated, surreal-
istic—but a more pedestrian style fits me better, since I am talking
about feelings common to most members of the Human Alliance; it
was only me who has been so shy about it all until now.

Mary, I have described you to myself as well as to some of my
friends in terms I never used before. (Why, even you would call that
infatuation although I don't "fatuate in" easily—or at all.) I feel you
to be complementary to me—making me whole, at peace with the
world, with myself; making me want to touch you not just with the
touch of lust but with the fingers of inquiry and inquisitiveness, in
search of the Marvellous Magnificent (the incredible) and of the
serene and reticent as well, and the coolness of your skin and the
firmness of your buttocks give me immediate answers to questions
perhaps even Solomon in his wisdom could not divine.

Well, you are my Sulamith anyway—although your hair has a
reddish glint and the arc of your nose is Tuscan, not Hebrew.

I am aware of you at the cardinal points of your absence as I
approach/reproach them. When you sit beside me dressed/undressed
I don't want to tell the difference. How could I have known that a
virgin is at times woman to the fourth power? (Or the fifth, sixth, and
seventh power, i.e., more power to you my love, my slender bride.)

Why am I telling you these things? I have no claim on you; you
are not like an arctic archipelago on which oilmen, gold diggers,
muskox hunters stake their claims; you belong to yourself—you
offer to me as much of your being as you feel just and justified.

You are the millstone, bread, and knife; press, wine and chalice.
You don't know how hungry and thirsty I am—one camps in the
desert and becomes queasy with sand.

It is St. Valentine's Day and this is a kind of Valentinian message. It should be written in the snow, on your palms and on the soles of your feet:

Accept me for I have accepted you (always) and if you incline your head a little

I'll be able to kiss your nape

which is what I planned all along anyway.

*George*

\*\*\*

## February 22nd

*My darling,*

It is as if I were compelled to write to you; to make use of the coded language to record, summarize, to build and embellish essentially simple ideas which concern you; my unabashed physical desire for your flooding loins and my continuing fascination & amazement at your overdrive intellect and barometric sensitivity.

The closeness of your flesh relaxes & excites me: it is as it should be—as it had been in my fantasies long ago—fantasies I thought I abandoned as excess luggage, as burdensome bric-a-brac only to recover/rediscover them at customs check in the interminable terminal of Melfi Airport ...

What can I say? I approach you as a gardener steps up to a newly blooming yet unnamed rose touching (you, it?) with a gentle hand opening the petals (one by one—almost) of a flower not to be cut or broken, but to grow and hold her head above all other plants in the garden. For you are opening your inner hold for your own pleasure as well as for mine; how could I hurt you? I want happiness for you, the kind all humans are entitled to, but few ever get. Not because they are incapable of experiencing it but because they don't allow themselves to accept the intensity of joy, ecstasy, or even the quiet glow of things going well. How could you be guilty of anything? I like your innocence sprinkled on lust—for the pure all things are pure—or so says St. Paul.

I would like you now to sit on my lap. But you do it without my asking; naturally with the easy grace of one moving on familiar terrain; (you fit oh so well in the curve of my body/ now you make my body your garden—touch me and I bloom, speak to me and I rearrange my paths and patches; at once you have miraculous powers not over but within me—use them!)

I can't finish this letter—it continues in my head and I'll keep sending it to you; ever changing but essentially with the same message: I love you (in the abbreviated eternity of our lives)—I want you beside me so that I could touch the simple miracle of your existence knowing that through your delightful smile our region of the universe was made just a bit more comprehensible.

    *G*

***

### Nemesvita, Hungary

How is this possible? I sit on the porch of Andras' house; a peasant cottage really—brought up to standards: a Western bathroom, no less—lights everywhere, computer, fridge, and a brown mouse in surprised attendance. A garden: fragrant grapes, ripe tomatoes, peaches & pears, eye-blue plums fallen on yellow clay; clumps of grass, all under those dark-green hills—almost Mediterranean. Massive Mount St. George a mile away; the lake a faint steel-gray glitter.

How is this possible, that I love you so suddenly with an intensity so unlike the mild beauty of this late Hungarian summer that your absence frightens me so: a blood clot or a bad driver might slide between us forever? How is it possible, this feeling, this confession to the self? (Perhaps hearing dead J pleading with living J in precise Hungarian tones—read eons ago onto a forlorn tape made me reflect.) I have no tapes, no monument in time—how would you ever know what I've always felt. The fantasy, firing the impersonal act cannot convey it; cannot print out the indescribable: That which belongs to the one who belongs.

At night the North Star stands almost above this semi-neglected yard among thatched roofs—vineyards up & down the slopes. Here gnarled old folks speak with the accents of my indestructible aunt in my own county, in my own land. And I am not at home. I am at home with you. Where you are. And once I'm dead I'll be forever homeless.

*G*

\*\*\*

## Nuns' Island, Montreal

To: *The Unnamed Flower*
From: *The gardener*

This is a letter of extreme urgency, that is, it has been travelling at the speed of light throughout the centuries and it has been arriving at your mailbox for the last thousand years. This is a letter also about the creeping
LONELINESS & BLAH
which only your blossoming presence can dispel BECAUSE
This has been one of your preordained tasks that you SOOTHE (*Soulager aussi*) the anxiety about existence (a totally ridiculous concern for all will die willy-nilly) and tolerate and NEUTRALIZE certain vicious outbursts as do rare plants which counteract hideous poisons; I submit to your love, for it is the one impossible gift, the one incomprehensible & sustained act of redemption that lifts the cleansing of soul (also plural) out of the chilled gothic of bishopric form into one (mine) secular & despairing life; wave your petals & similes, open your images, prayerbooks, loins (*pas lointain*) for I need

saving in this world, never mind eternity who cares about eternity when your body is imprinted into mine; a kinaesthetic memory—I demand a miracle a sustained miracle of your presence; I am a supplication, an offering, a holy & unholy tantrum; I want your love, I am lost & condemned without it; (probably even with it, but with it it is more tolerable) there is a shamelessness in me to confront you like this, but what the hell ... I am my own wreath, dedication and monument; for you I would prepare a garden of delights, delicacies, cadences & decadences even; I want to overwhelm you as you have overshadowed me in salty spasms and tightened yourself around my probes. It is late at night that I am writing this; the night has a marvellous disinhibiting effect; I feel I must have your raw closeness, a smell of soap, urine, sweat & other animal excreta slightly modified by perfume; I address you with my body you must listen, because

BLAST IT I DESERVE YOUR LOVE

Inreturn I giveyouonethousand rosescolouredtospecifications andexoticcigarettesexcept youdonotsmoke andpornographicpic-turesbut yourimaginationoutstripsthem(punintended) andmyself-giftwrappedwithapinkribbonaroundmy ohmy

what I really want to say is that I accept you as you are;
I will gladly accept you as my wife
but I will be satisfied with your companionship
in this plasticine eternity
without legal tangles
as you desire.

As I am closing my eyes I'd like to conjure your image, but instead small streams glitter; mountains draw the charts of the spring offensive against the blue paper of an uncertain Northern sky, and my daughter is drinking from an unpolluted creek.

Your image is on my skin, it is in my muscles, in my taste buds; I don't have to visualize you to associate you with what I hold valuable. The images were of today's. Your memory ("the memory of you" as popular songs would have it) leaps across the skeletal embers of yesterday and twirls a proverbial red scarf across the screen with the opening bars of an unrecognized song about an unnamed flower which blossoms in an almost indescribable garden every Wednesday & Sunday until further notice.

I ask for your forgiveness the way as some polite surgeons ask the same from their nurses, beforehand, concerning their outbursts during an operation. It may well be that we are engaged in an important & delicate operation. The patient must surely be allowed to live.

G

\*\*\*

## Budapest, Hungary

*Dear Mary,*
I'm surrounded by indescribable beauty and friendship. I'm sending you my love & desire & I'm missing you terribly. I wish you were here with my friends who received me to great love & understanding. My greetings to Julian & Stephan.

Your devoted husband & lover,
*George*

In the Dead of Winter

# WHAT IS THIS THING
# CALLED LOVE?

Year Nine

# 27

The backyard is a sea of snow. I would have better luck walking on water.

Snow: the booby prize for living in this cold land, Kanada. Winter is like a friend who has turned his back on you. A turncoat. A traitor to the cause: your happiness.

A lit fireplace in mid-winter generates the same generosity of spirit as does a garden in mid-summer; each sparkle: the lord of the dance. But I don't have a fireplace. I don't have much.

I can turn to the mirror and be damned, or I can turn to a friend … And here she is … Olga is in front of my house, but the snow has piled up, and she can't reach my door. Why haven't I shovelled the snow?

"My husband always did it," I tell her. "I can't get used to doing it. Even after his cancer had returned and he was having chemotherapy treatments, he shovelled the snow. The illness didn't change him, but it changed me. I gave up on him."

"You did no such thing. When he became bedridden most wives would have opted for hospice care, but you took care of him at home."

"He was a good patient. After I changed him, he'd say: 'That felt so good. I like having my ass cleaned. You're my angel.' But I was no angel. I didn't resent the work involved, but I did resent the expense. Disposable underwear costs a fortune."

"George made the best of a bad situation. He knew he was dying, and accepted it."

"Dying was not on his to-do-list. A week before he died, a palliative care doctor asked him: 'How are you?' and he said: 'I'm fine. Why shouldn't I be?' Supposedly you go through five distinct stages to cope with a terminal illness—from denial to anger to bargaining to acceptance—but not him. Denial is a good coping mechanism. It helped him, but not me. I hated the anxiety of not knowing—would he live another week, another month—a year? I didn't want him to die, but I can't say I wanted him to live either."

"Of course you wanted him to live," she says.

She is certain I was a good wife, but was I?

"When you lose the most important person in your life, nothing else matters," she says. "When my grandfather died, my grandmother stopped speaking. She became a mute."

"Something similar happened to one of George's patients—he stopped hearing. 'Hysterical deafness'—he called it. George liked difficult cases. And not necessarily because he was kind or good-hearted but rather, because he was an intellectual at heart. He diagnosed an illness, and then, like the good intellectual or mind-surgeon that he was, he aimed to remove whatever anxieties or fears the individual had. The procedure was an intellectual exercise, and in fact, it had to be for the therapy to work. He couldn't become emotionally involved; otherwise he would do more harm than good."

"He was a good therapist," she says.

I agree. "After he became bedridden, he was nicer to me than ever. At night, when I tucked him into bed, he would often ask: 'Do you love me?' I hesitated before I answered ... I had the stupid idea that I would be better off without him."

"You're torturing yourself—and for no good reason," Olga tells me. While she makes herself a cup of tea, I decidedly make myself miserable, remembering how stupid I was ...

Stupid me: Before my husband died I figured when it did happen I would get a cat and be comforted. I did get a cat, but it didn't do much. Stupid me: I thought if I had a new mattress, I would sleep better. (I don't.)

One day the house belonged to George and Mary, and now it belongs only to Mary ... Stupid me: Before my husband died I thought I would be pleased by the sole ownership—doubling my net worth. When my husband used to say towards the end of his life, "our" house, I used to smile and think to myself it's not "our" house but "my" house. And now that it is "my" house, I look around, and think so this is my Empire of Dust. What irony, the thing I longed for—financial independence—I get it and it means nothing.

Everyone assumes money makes the world go round and then when someone they love passes away, they realize money doesn't do much. They expect to be awarded a Certificate in Enlightenment—how stupid is that?

Stupid me: I expect the dead to speak. What would my late husband say if he could talk to me? Would he tell me: "The more we know, the less we know?" Or would he be more forthright in his condemnation? He might stand by my window and belt out Cole Porter's "What Is This Thing Called Love?" It's not a happy tune. The crooner tells his object of desire: "I saw you there one wonderful day; you took my heart and threw it away." That's what I did—I threw his love away. I waited for him to die so I could be free. Free to do what?

Olga checks the weather report on the internet. Another winter storm is brewing.

"If there is a blackout," she says, "you can put your perishables outside."

Snow: Mother Nature's fridge—top of the line; eco-friendly. Snow: corpse-friendly.

I tell my friend: "George had asked me to keep the urn interred with his ashes in the house, and I had said yes, but then as he had donated his body to McGill University, I would have had to fork out $1,500 for them. I couldn't do it. Besides, where would I have kept the urn? On a bookshelf? In the cupboard? I got spooked."

"That would spook anybody."

"Not George. Nothing spooked him. Four days before he died—on Monday night—he woke up laughing. He apologized for waking me up but said he couldn't help it. A group of Hungarians had been in the room and had told him a joke."

"That man liked to laugh. And eat! And he adored you."

"He might have, but not anymore. I expected he would show up in my dreams—visit me—but he hasn't."

"And he won't. That sort of thing doesn't happen," she says, looking at me strangely. Who in their right mind wants to be haunted? I do! I do. I want my dead husband to stand before me and absolve me of my sins.

The moment my friend leaves, the silence is so loud the noise of the TV does not drum it out. I long for my husband to be in the room with me. Those last few days of his life he did not say much, but his presence had a calming effect. The sound of his breathing had a spiritual overtone—kind of like the sound of a mountain brook or a Bach sonata.

Grieving is akin to being wrapped up in a linen burial cloth. You see the world through the slits in the cloth. Even when the lights are on (all the lights in my house are on!), you don't see much. That's why you return to the past. Once upon a time the world was new & glorious & fun-filled & colourful, and now, it's not.

# 28

Ding dong.

At the door are a pair of husky, government-paid workers, here to pick up the hospital bed, the wheelchair, the walker and the cane once used by my dear old husband.

I show the men in, and they immediately set to remove all traces of how my late husband was artfully tortured by Cancer in this very room. The day the Torturer did him in, men, just like these two, wrapped him up in plastic, and put him in a body bag.

Ding dong.

At the door: the repairman for the furnace. Watch your step ... Come right in; the electricity is turned off ...

Ding dong.

At the door: some guy who delivers pizzas. Wrong address.

Someone (who?) asks: "Mary, Mary quite contrary, how does your garden grow?"

I don't know the answer. I don't even know who is asking the question. Is it my late husband?

All I am sure of is that the hospital bed, the wheelchair, the walker, and the cane that my late husband used are gone for good, and I miss them. I knew I would miss my husband once he passed away, but who would ever thought I could miss the hospital bed he lay on? Sounds kind of silly, but so it is.

Someone (who?) asks: "Mary, Mary, quite contrary, how does your garden grow?"

We're in the dead of winter, damn it. There is no garden. And I miss it. I miss my garden like I would miss a finger or a toe if it were accidentally cut off; I wouldn't dare say I miss it like I would a hand or a foot—that would be an outrageous statement, though in my gloom, I do think it.

I would miss the books I have read in my life if I hadn't gotten round to opening their covers and giving myself over to them. I would miss the roof on my house if it weren't there to protect me from the rain, the snow and the big bad wolf (the wind), so too I miss my garden ... But what of it?

Ding dong ... Your conscience calling: "Mary, Mary quite contrary, if you had taken better care of your husband, had been a better wife, God would have allowed him to stay on a little longer. It is your fault he didn't keep his day job—loving you."

Ding dong ... No one is at the door. I am hearing things. Just my imagination on fire ... Where is everyone?

I miss my garden though not half as much as I miss having my late aunts and uncles round the dinner table. Are they breaking bread in another part of the universe (call it heaven)? If only I could have absolute faith that they are doing just that. (There is life after death!) All I am sure of is that time is beating me up and that this is no way to treat a lady. I miss my garden like I miss my youth, well, maybe not as much as that, but I do miss it as much as I miss my youthful complexion.

Before the cold weather set in I used to rush to my garden; it wasn't a needle in a haystack I was looking for, but my peace of mind. Strangely, or not so strangely, I often found it ...

My little garden was a Holy Shrine to what I could be—I could be happy. My garden was a magical shrine in the little hills of a forgotten country, I visited it when I was down in the dumps, and now it's nowhere to be seen. Pilgrims to the shrines of the Virgin Mary bring bouquets of wild flowers, courting her good favour; my little shrine in the virgin hills of Yesterday presented me with flowers en masse and now it's gone. It fenced in my appetite for self-destruction, and now it's nowhere to be seen. I am at the mercy of the Prince of Darkness.

If only the winter could fly South, if only I could erase the next three months off the calendar, if only I could magically transport myself to Australia or New Zealand (it would have to be magic, I can't afford a plane ticket), if only I could find myself in a warm climate and be happy.

Here I am rambling off when all I wanted to do was to stop and take note of how I miss my pretty garden, how I miss being of use, and how I miss being Mary, the able Gardener, the wise lady of Grand Blvd. I miss, of course, being wife to the late Dr. Nemeth, healer and famed Hungarian poet: Vitez Gyorgy.

Years ago I wished for a new kind of life—an adventure or two; a meaningful job I could spring out of my bed for. Years ago I had no idea that if you had a garden and a loving husband you had it all. I once had it all, and didn't know it.

Everyone is in need of a miracle or two. Those who bring their troubles to the Virgin Mary expect long-term solutions, or solace at the minimum. I brought my troubles to my garden, and sought short-term help for my constant, eerie descent into the backwaters of self-depreciation, and now it's nowhere to be seen, as is my one true love.

# 29

You don't expect to be in a traffic accident when you get into a car. You don't expect to be in an earthquake or a flood when you go on vacation. You don't expect tragedy to enter your life. You don't expect sadness to overwhelm you when you get a long-distance phone call, but when someone on the other end tells you out of the blue that someone you love dearly has died quite unexpectedly, what do you do?

The grief counsellor, heading the self-help group I am participating in, is not sure how to answer the question directed at her.

"Expect pain," she finally says, offering the woman a Kleenex. "Expect to cry yourself to sleep. It's inevitable. Every night I can hear my next door neighbour cry himself to sleep. His wife died more than a year ago, and still he cries."

A twice-widowed seventy-year-old raises his hand and says: "After my wife died, death became less scary."

Another member of the group, a widow, a woman in her seventies, says that her life was over when her husband died. He died twelve years ago and she still can't manage to overcome the sorrow. Like waking up from a car accident and finding out the driver of the other vehicle is dead, being a widow lasts forever. You can never put the incident behind you.

"The word 'widow' is a powerful social marker," the grief counsellor admits.

Don't I know it! When I got married my status went up—from Miss to Mrs., and now I am somewhere in between—not quite married, and not quite single—an ambiguous state. No one is going around calling me Widow Mary to my face, but I feel they are thinking it. No one has called me Mrs. Nemeth for weeks.

An older woman in the group, a teacher, who recently lost her younger sister to cancer, notes it has become socially unacceptable to talk about death. It's a taboo subject. Living in a secular society, where the emphasis is on staying in the moment, death is a hindrance to The Good Life. Nowadays you're not supposed to say someone died, but rather that he "passed." The word "passed" has positive connotations. It's the word that is used when a child passes an exam, or passes a school year.

"The vocabulary surrounding death and dying has changed," the grief counsellor admits, "but this is not necessarily a bad thing. The need for solace is not to be sneered at. In the past religion helped ease the tension, and now without it, there's no relief."

The group agrees. Whether you're rich or poor, educated or uneducated, whether you're naturally good-natured or a grouch, whether you're a sweet young thing or a golden oldie, death takes you by surprise and makes you feel like shit. (That may sound coarse, but then that's how it is!)

A lovely 30-something, whose pre-school children can't understand why their father isn't coming home, tells the group that the first major holidays on her own were difficult to get through, but there were other firsts which were just as unpleasant. Getting through the first snowstorm of the year also made her list of horrors. She had prepared herself for the pain that comes with the big events, she had built up her defenses, but she had not prepared herself for something as minor as weathering the first snowstorm by herself. This is a cold country, and it's much colder without a husband.

The twice-divorced widower says that he had a dream in which his late wife called him on the phone and told him that she was OK. That comforted him.

A woman my age, of Italian origin, tells us: "Two nights after my husband died I saw him at the foot of my bed. He looked just as he always did, except younger. He told me: 'I love you forever and ever. Nothing can stop me from protecting you.'"

Her words invoke jealousy. Her husband visited her, and mine did not. Her husband must care for her a lot more than mine does. I yearn for him to drop by like an orphan yearns for his parents to show up and take care of him, or like someone who is paralyzed yearns to walk again, but all my yearning gets me nowhere. I'm left to my own devices.

The group might have an opinion on whether or not it is reasonable to expect a dead person to visit you, but the session is over. This particular health care agency offers eight sessions, and this is number seven. I suffered the loss of a husband, and now, in a month's time, I will have to suffer the loss of this support group.

Participating in a bereavement self-help group warms you up— for real. It's kind of like entering an igloo when there is a storm raging outside. An igloo is made of snow and ice; the material is cold, and yet it shelters those in it. When I am part of this group, I feel less alone; less inclined to self-abuse. But there is nothing to be done—the session is over. Goodnight ...

The sidewalks are slippery and the snow is piling up on the streets. Widows, young widows, old widows, it's all the same— we're all walking down the street with dead husbands. People see the imagined ghosts of our dead husbands, and become afraid. Their husbands could die, too.

What to do ...?

The twice-widowed individual, the 70-year-old fellow, catches up to me at the bus stop and assures me that it's-better-to-have-loved-and-lost-than-never-to-have-loved.

He asks: "How many years were you married?"

"Thirty-four," I tell him.

"That's more than I was," he says.

I gloat. Sports fishermen weigh in their catch hoping for that coveted once-a-year trophy that will advertise their skill and good fortune; widows and widowers do the same—they place the number of years they have been married on a scale and examine their catch. Prizes are given out to those who have been married the longest.

The widower tells me that, when he lost his first wife, it hurt like hell, when he lost his second wife, that hurt too, but not nearly as much as the first time. And not because he loved her less, but because he knew it would be possible to find another partner.

"You don't have to be alone," he says, putting his arm around my shoulder.

I pull myself away. I don't want any man to touch me. I need a year of cleansing. I have to pay for my sins. The sin of living while my husband is dead.

The 70-year-old goes his way, and I go mine. I am confident he will find Wife No. 3. I know the statistics. Most widowers re-marry within three years, but only one out of eight widows manage to do it.

There is a cosmic law at work—nothing lasts. Is the universe God's idea of installation art? And if it is, is it worthy of rave reviews? God could have done better. In a well-made universe couples would not have to wait to be re-united after death; there would be no death.

That voice in my head (is it the late Dr. George Nemeth?) tells me: "A true artist doesn't give a damn about what others think of his work. That annoys critics, but in the long run, it's for the best. (Think of Van Gogh and his unexpected rise to the top!) Turn to the mirror and think of it as a frame, and yourself as a living work of art."

I can't ever imagine looking at a mirror and being pleased ... What gives me pleasure is looking at pictures of my late husband. A chalice provides sustenance to a priest, pictures of my late husband do it for me. The pillow he died on also provides comfort. Often, I put my head on it, and am pleased. You would think sorrow is a bed of nails, but sometimes, amazingly it brings comfort.

# 30

Those who once stood on the shores of The River Jordan and broke bread with the young Jesus had the good fortune of being handed loaves of mercy; when I visit my aging parents I too am offered spiritual sustenance. Even though my father is living in a nursing home, and the place is not all that nice, when I am with him and my mother, the little girl in me feels twice-blessed. Not only does my mother provide an array of Italian dishes fit for a king, but my father, who when I was growing up was rather cold towards me, now isn't. Confined to a wheelchair, my father, a victim of Parkinson's, can't remember much, but somehow he has not forgotten my husband is dead and because of it he is forever gracious and tender and gentle and super kind to me.

"Have some more lasagna," my mother tells me and I oblige, knowing there isn't a resident at this nursing home that wouldn't exchange his prepared mush for my mother's twice-baked, home-cooked lasagna noodles.

My mother could turn a soup kitchen into a top-rated Italian restaurant, that's how good a cook she is. But then it's hard to say how accurate my assessment is of her cooking abilities—when I am with her this little miracle called self-love surfaces, and I am content. I can't say I'm happy, happy is too big a word, but I am free of grief and that's not nothing. In her presence if I have a headache, I'm confident it's not a brain tumour. (An aspirin will take care of it.) She has a magic hold on me—things will work out.

Like other Italian immigrants who eagerly crossed the Atlantic Ocean in the late 1950s and resettled in North America, my mother proved it's possible to move up. In Italy she lived in a little hut with no running water, no amenities of any kind, constantly worried she would go hungry, and now she lives in a nice enough place, having more food than she knows what to do with. Dreams come true—well, they did—for her generation.

Is death a simple passage from one place to another? And if it is, is my late husband nicely settled in, or does he feel like a refugee—out of place, out of tune and nostalgic for his house on Grand Blvd.?

My mother is certain those in heaven have no wish to return to this world. In fact, her next door neighbours, Angelo and his two sons, all three who had died within a few years of each other, collaborated this for her.

"The other day," she tells me, "at the crack of dawn, Angelo and his two sons stood at the foot of my bed. Rocco, the younger of the two sons, told me: 'This place where we are is so beautiful. *La Terra per Sempere,* The Land that Is Forever, is the best possible. The world we came from does not compare. All is vanity there, people trying to outdo each other. Here no one criticizes each other, no one is richer or poorer than anyone else. In *La Terra per Sempere* all of us are happy.'"

"It was just a dream," I say.

"I was fully awake. I was about to get up."

I believe her.

If my mother's neighbours (who passed away about a decade ago) could visit her at the crack of dawn, why can't my late husband visit me?

The unthinkable happened—my husband has not only dared to die and left me to fend for myself, but unlike other men, newly dead, who have the audacity to visit their ladies' chambers dressed in heavenly attire (which seem to be similar to our earthly ones), my husband has not paid me a visit. I expected to wake up one night and find my dearest friend at the foot of my bed, but no such thing has happened ...

On a chair, not far from my father, close to the TV, sits an old woman who repeats the words: "Help me or kill me."

My father tries to get out of his wheelchair to comfort the lady who vaguely looks like my late aunt, but he can't. He is strapped in.

He tells me: "I never hurt anyone. I did not do anything wrong to anyone. Why am I a prisoner? Why am I tied down in a chair? Why can't I go home? I am not dead."

"I thought you liked it here," my mother says, patting him on the head as if he were a naughty child.

And then when I am about to leave she offers me a large batch of my favourite things: almond biscotti, taralli and pizzelle. All of which she herself made, of course. Here are little edible miracles I can take home. Loot bags filled with absolution. (Mary, you were a good daughter, and a good wife—believe it!)

# 31

Winter is a key. It opens springtime ... Not so fast. Another snow storm is in the offing.

Linda, a friend and fellow advocate of flower power, is set to arrive from Calgary. If she had come in the summer there would have been flowers from my garden prominently displayed on the dining room table, but at this time of the year, I have no home-grown magic to offer her. Either a friend is missing, or my flowers are. (My husband always is.)

"Buy some flowers at a shop," Olga, my friend and Linda's as well, suggests.

I suppose going to a florist during a cold spell is akin to going to a therapist—it can only do you good. And yet ... Find me flowers and I won't buy them. It is not flowers I want this winter but the transformation of our city into a flower shop. May our mayor in his next life become a florist with magical powers and turn our Canadian March into an Australian one.

On the coldest day of the year going out to buy fresh flowers takes courage; how Olga and I manage it, I don't know, but somehow we do.

Flower shops make me think of red-light districts—everything can be had for a price. Flowers are like call girls—the fresher the product (or the more exotic), the higher the mark-up. Looking at pricey flowers in a florist shop is akin to catching the admiring glance of a good-looking man. Love at first sight? No way! Flowers let you take chances, men don't.

The saleslady at the flower shop explains that to prolong the life of cut flowers you have to choose those whose buds are just beginning to open rather than full blooms as the buds will last longer. The flowers have to be kept away from sun and stored at night in a cool, dark place. On the other hand if I really want something that lasts, I can always opt for a house plant.

House plants make me think of delinquent teens, needy and crying for attention. Besides, they take over the window, and I need all the sunlight I can get or I wilt. Know thyself, and act accordingly.

I choose a dozen carnations—their fragrance alone is worth the price—and a multitude of other floral treasures.

"Flowers fresh from the florist please me," I tell Olga, "but not as much as those I myself have grown. Why, I'm not sure, unless it's because I have the illusion of having mothered the flowers in my garden while those I buy at a shop I babysit."

"I never imagined when I was younger that I would take so much pleasure from gardening," Olga tells me, as eager as I am for spring to arrive and for the ground to thaw.

Our friend Linda who, despite the bad weather, manages to make it to my house, shares the same opinion—gardening is fun. Actually, it is more than fun. Like indulging in an extreme sport, gardening offers unique sensations and pleasures denied those who don't know the thrill of challenging the elements. Linda can't wait to return to her Calgary home where her spring bulbs are almost in bloom. (Thanks to this year's unusually warm chinook winds!)

Early flowering tulips are a show of force. They suggest rebirth is not only desirable, but well within the norm. Definite proof there is life after death, I let it be known.

"The night my mother died I thought I heard her coming up the stairs," Linda tells the two of us. "As she was then in the hospital, and I was at home, half-asleep in bed, that couldn't have been the case. Still, according to the medical reports, my mother passed away just around the time I heard those footsteps."

"I wish I could tell you I heard George's footsteps coming up the stairs after he died, but nothing of the sort happened. He has forgotten me."

"I doubt it," Olga says.

"Then why hasn't he contacted me and told me what I want to hear?"

Olga and Linda (buddies since college) look at me as if I had gone off the deep end. Don't I know it?—dead men don't speak. Still, I expected my dear old hubby to communicate to me telepathically and say something like: "My sweet Mary, I promise you that there are good things to come. Don't be afraid. Miss me, but not so much as to poison the joy of having arms, legs and a good pair of lungs—mobility. A lovely body all round. A true gift! Be kind to yourself, my darling, and I will do my best to look after you."

"George doted on you," Linda says. "You were everything to him."

I may have been, but not anymore. 'Cause if that man had any feelings for me he would have taken the trouble to leave his abode for a minute or two, knocked on my door and told me in no uncertain terms that he still loves me. But he hasn't. If only he would come and assure me that I am not alone on this dreary planet. Sure, this planet is not all that dreary for those who walk arm in arm with the love of their lives, but for those of us whose husbands are currently residing in another part of the universe, address unknown, this planet has lost its lustre, and that's all there is to it.

Each morning I make my way to the snow-filled backyard looking for inspiration, good tidings, coping strategies on how to deal with the fact that I am a widow. I expect that in-the-skull therapist to pop up and offer some sage advice like: "Be strong as a rock and feel no pain, or better yet, be strong and flexible as an evergreen and thrive." But I get nothing. The moment I return indoors, the Hit Man, Grief, drags me to the mirror and reminds me that once upon a time I was Dr. George Nemeth's wife and beloved sex object, but no more. Grief will do me in (a given). The Good Doctor is not around to protect me. He is not around to warn me: "Turn to the mirror and be prepared to feel inadequate. The mirror will not help you, help yourself. If you want a tutorial on self-reliance turn to a lake and go fishing." Each morning I confront the mirror like I would a Hit Man—I look the other way. (In terror!)

Preparing lunch, I tell Linda and Olga: "A few days before George died, eating the soft-boiled egg I had made, he told me: 'The whole world should know how good eggs are! They contain everything a person needs.' I had no idea then that this would be his last meal. That was Monday. On Friday, at 11:50 a.m., I noticed he wasn't breathing. 'Wake up,' I shouted at him, and when he didn't, I pinched him. Even after he had died, I was telling him what to do."

"Mary, you never told George what to do, and if you did, he never listened to you," Olga says.

"That's true. He was a free spirit. He didn't take anything seriously. He loved to laugh. To his mind laughter was the fountain of youth, and it didn't cost a penny. Gardening also helped you stay young, but it wasn't as cost-effective. Still, he spent half his day in the backyard, tending to his vegetables."

Both Linda and Olga agree: the backyard is The place to be. Each new season brings in its own style, and classic good looks. It comes with a message: You don't have to age gracefully—you can do better than that. Old is sexy. Sure it is. Just look at how nature reinvents itself—surprising us, amusing us, titillating us, changing colours, changing attitudes and moods as well. Now that's entertainment! Even in mid-January a crocus or an iris can show up in your backyard and make you feel as if you had just hit the jackpot. You're rich! If Heaven has a national currency, it might be flowers.

As a gardener you have to believe the future is rosy. Babies are prized long before they make their appearance; so too are spring bulbs. Call it an act of faith, rather than a leap of faith. The mother of all lessons: What you are looking for can be found right in your own backyard (or front yard for that matter).

Celebrate the simple pleasures in life with a friend or two and you win first prize. Which is ...?

An hour or so without grief.

A cool breeze, the sight of a pretty flower, going to a museum or taking in a movie can be comforting, but if you are in the company of a friend or two, well then, you have an advantage. Grief, the Hit Man, can't pull the trigger. In the company of a friend or two, you are certain (well, almost certain) that you are an integral part of the universe, and not an outsider looking in, a pitiful dog of a woman whose spirit was maliciously cut up into a thousand little pieces. In their company you are ready (well, almost ready) to turn to the mirror as a child turns to his toy box.

Love can undo curses. (The curse of being lonely.) Love can take away hexes. Change bad luck into good luck.

Outside—snow. Inside: daisies & a slew of other heavenly artefacts. Outside—a storm is brewing. Inside: coffee & conversation. Someone says (Who?): "Turn to the mirror looking for compliments, and you'll be in for a fall. Best to turn to a friend who sugar-coats the truth."

# The Last Days of Winter

# MARY, WHAT IS ...?

## Year Nine

# 32

I see my late husband at the foot of the bed.

"You came, you actually came to visit me," I tell him. I am so happy to see him. He looks neither young nor old; he is in his mid-40s.

I say to him: "Kiss me."

He comes closer, but just as he is about to kiss me, I say: "What is it like where you are? Is it an al-ter-na-tive (alternate) reality?"

I don't pronounce the word, "alternate" very well. He doesn't seem to understand what it is I am asking. This surprises me because my late husband would immediately recognize my mispronunciations.

He gets on top of me; he feels very heavy. I think—if he is a spirit, I shouldn't feel his weight, something is wrong here. And then he says: "My arm hurts; there is so much pain in my arm." His body starts to disintegrate, piece by piece. I get frightened ... Suddenly I am walking outside. A little girl says to me: "He was born in 1603."

I wake up. I remember the dream; it's not the dream I wish I had had. It upsets me. Was it my husband who actually visited me? Or was it an impostor?

I pull up the blind. Another record-breaking cold day. But the sunshine pours in. Unlike Hydro Quebec, the sun does not bill me for services rendered. I should count my blessings, but how can I? I miss my late husband too much. I miss him like a person undergoing amputation would miss having anaesthesia. I miss him like a heroin addict misses her fix. No—not that. Love can't be compared to a drug addiction. That would be like saying plants need the sun and that's their addiction. Plants have the right to sunlight, and I have the right to love.

If only I could shout across the galaxy and call out to my husband, but I can't. All I can do is get on with my day. On the agenda: a lecture on "The History of Rock and Roll" at McGill University's Life Long Learning Program for retirees.

Days pass, and then weeks. On the morning of February 9ᵗʰ I wake up and hear my late husband speaking to me in his distinctive, thick Hungarian accent. He says to me: "Mary, what is …?"

Here I have been waiting for communication from him for so long, and then what do I get? A question! An incomplete question at that. Was he asking (as he often did): "Mary, what is for supper?" Or was he simply quoting *the last words* of one his favourite writers, Gertrude Stein? On her deathbed she asked: "What is the answer?" And when no one replied, she laughed and responded herself: "Then what is the question?"

Perplexed. Days and weeks go by … And then I find myself in what looks similar to a hospital waiting room. There are two parts to it. On one side people can walk through walls, and on the other side, they can't. I find myself with my late husband in the area where people can walk through walls. When I wake up, I feel good, but not for long, because I have another dream, and in it my late husband says to me: "We were never suited for each other. We should get a divorce." I cry like I never cried before. Here I was, as certain of my late husband's love as I was that I had ten fingers and had given birth to two sons, and now, this.

I always believed when I died my late husband would come round and he would take me to the Otherworld. But what if he was now in love with someone else—someone nicer, prettier, and smarter than me? What if he has forgotten me altogether and I will be on my own? That would be hell.

I try to shake off the bad dream, but I can't. I look for signs that it was a big mistake … And then two weeks later a fellow classmate at McGill tells me: "I adore you. You are my angel."

These are the exact words my late husband used to say to me. Is he speaking to me through this man?

I assure the retired professor that I can't be his angel as he doesn't know me.

He replies: "You have such beautiful, sensual lips. I would like the company of an attractive woman. We could tell each other secrets. Hold hands and kiss. I am an open book, do you want to read it?"

Considering my advanced years, and my Oh-So-Ordinary-Looks, why would anyone say something like this to me? Unless, of course, it was my late husband who was trying to get word to me.

Days ... weeks go by. And then I find myself in a big city, much like New York, except it is quiet—there are no cars on the road. I enter an office—it has long rows of desks. My late husband is sitting at a desk writing notes. (No computers in evidence.) I have the feeling he is a university professor and this is his office. He introduces me as his wife to a colleague. He kisses me. I ask him: "Why don't you come home? Why do we have to live apart?" And he says: "There was too much noise at home. We have to live apart but I still love you."

Those words of love comfort me and yet I wonder if I can believe them. It was just a dream—wasn't it? What would my late husband and sometime therapist say to all this? Would he tell me that what I was experiencing was what psychologists call "survivor's guilt"? And that with the passage of time the anxiety and depression associated with it would diminish? Possibly. Would he analyse my dreams? Unlikely. (He didn't put much scope in that kind of thing.)

Luckily, he wrote down his ideas on how to effectively make a business of your mental health. I read his self-help guide and it makes me feel better.

# Some Suggestions To Live By

*(Prepared for a patient by G.A. Nemeth, Ph.D.)*

1. Never give up on a cause you truly believe in.
2. Don't put yourself down.
3. Build up and maintain self-confidence; you deserve trusting yourself.
4. Assert yourself in all situations. Don't be a doormat; nor should you be aggressive. Throwing tantrums or grovelling are the opposite of self-assertion.
5. Accept others as *they are*. You are free to associate with them— or avoid them as you see fit.
6. Don't be afraid of making mistakes. If you feel you've done your best and things don't work out, it's not your fault.
7. Don't be afraid in general. It just makes you feel sick and helpless.
8. Allow yourself to love others; allow others to love you.
9. Trust, but not blindly. (In Latin: *Fide, sed cui, vide.*)
10. Focus on the hope of living, not on the fear of dying. A brave person dies only once; the coward dies a thousand deaths.
11. Life is a free gift from God's garage sale. Look, search and you may be lucky enough to find something of value even on a roadside table each day.
12. Celebrate Hope at the end of each day. Say: "*I survived; therefore I won today. I hope to win tomorrow also.*"

*A regal person does all these things with dignity, self-control, kindness and confidence.*

# 33

Every winter church bazaars have a list of goodies on sale. They include baked goods, home-made jams, nearly-new clothes, faith, hope and charity. The volunteer sales staff spend a lot of time behind the counter, twiddling their thumbs, waiting for someone called Jesus to buy their stuff, as there are not too many customers (no men at all!) to buy their handiwork. On occasion you will find a few ladies, like my friend and I, hounding church basements looking for bargains.

My friend, a bachelorette, suggests that in this lovely country of ours there is an over-abundance of stuff, but a scarcity of single older men. Either they're happily married or they're newly dead. What to do?

Self-pity is not sexy. A thought. Another thought: It's not difficult to be charitable in a country where fruits and vegetables are cheap.

A church lady offers me a sampling of her home-made goodies. "My husband loves my blueberry jam," she says, with the emphasis on *my* husband. Her wedding band is studded with diamonds.

Married ladies parade their gold bands with the same fervour patriots parade the American flag. Older women, younger women too, flaunt the words, "my husband," convinced that God is on "their" side. It's not that they shouldn't be proud of their marital status, but it's as if they were deliberately trying to invoke envy. They act like big-time contributors to charity events. The Bible says the rich shouldn't flaunt their good works, but often they do. Like a mother of six flaunts her young troops, like an A student flaunts her accomplishments to a friend who isn't so lucky in the brains department, married women flaunt their status to old-time spinsters and the like. Are they doing it out of maliciousness? Not at all—they're simply doing it, well, because, why shouldn't they?

"Didn't you do the same?" my friend asks.

"I did," I admit. Those who heard my flaunting possibly assumed that "my" husband was some Cary-Grant-look-alike. (He wasn't.)

Freud suggested women suffer from "penis envy." Whether or not they do is a hot topic for debate, but what Freud failed to note is that there are loads of women who suffer from "husband envy." And I am one such broad. I envy women with husbands like a woman living in a refugee camp envies a rich relative in America. How can someone have so much, and another have so little? Penis envy. Baby envy. Big breast envy. Slim figure envy ...

And then there goes that voice in my head. (Is it my late husband and sometime therapist, Dr. George Nemeth?): "Envy offers nothing but grief. Gluttons can satisfy their craving with food. But envy—what does it get you? Do yourself a favour—replace envy with admiration and you'll make yourself feel good."

If only it were that easy ...

My friend tells me that, before she retired, working as she did as a business executive, she was always thrown into the company of men. Actually, there were more men doing her job than women, so she never felt the lack of a man, especially being young and good looking; men were always after her. Back then she used to love being with her female friends as much as she used to love her job, prancing around the world. But now that the man she loved and refused to marry married someone else, deciding he wanted to be a father more than anything else in the world, she is on her own.

Everywhere she goes, she says, she is surrounded by women; she sometimes feels she is living in a nunnery. Or in a Macbeth play, and she is one of the witches. Nuns and witches. She might be better off with drug addicts and off-beat individuals than these suburban types—on the whole married women who love nothing better than complaining about their husbands. Even church ladies, those who exhort to love-others-as-themselves, spend more time admonishing their better halves than cherishing them.

"Going to an all-girl event is like going to a bar and finding out no alcoholic beverages are served," she says. "Such events are full of talk of sex, but no sex happens. When you are a single woman with heterosexual leanings, you are not looking for sweet young things in tight jeans; you are looking for a man who has the strength of an angel—his wing span is so great you can fly south real quick, if you get my meaning."

"I get it alright. Before my husband died I couldn't wait to be with my girlfriends and talk the night away. Now that I don't have a husband to return to, I don't enjoy women's company all that much. I hadn't expected this to happen. I had assumed after my husband died I would seek them out, needy for attention, but while I am needy, it's not them I want, but my dearly departed spouse."

"Would you have an affair with a married man?" she asks, indicating that just the previous week, a repairman (with a ring on his finger), asked her out on a date. He told her right away that his business was in his wife's name, as was his house, so he could not leave his wife no matter what might happen between them.

"I can't imagine ever wanting another woman's husband," I tell her. "That would be like borrowing a designer outfit; you have to take special care you don't damage it. It's too much of an ordeal if you ask me. I'd rather buy something cheap or second-hand. Personally, I don't even like flirting with married men."

"Other women's husbands like to flirt and you know why?" she asks.

"I have no idea."

"They want you to want them, and then, when you do, they inevitably tell their wives. Their wives' jealousy fuels their self-respect. (Like, they're hot property!)"

So here is yet another reason to avoid married guys. I can't imagine myself watching a TV show with any married man, let alone, undressing and showing what I have, or don't have ...

The two of us move from one area of the church basement to another, looking for that low-priced, high-quality one-of-a-kind item.

"How nice you look today," one of church ladies behind the sales counter tells me, and then turns around, and says the exact same thing to another older gal who doesn't look all that nice to me.

It seems older gals (me too) always greet each other by exclaiming: "What a nice dress!" Or asking: "New hairdo?" (It's enough you notice something is new, it doesn't seem to matter if you like it or not, everyone assumes you do, by the simple fact you noticed!) Young gals are generally honest with each other, but older gals (me too) take pride in being civil. We have mastered the art of hypocrisy to a T. But then the line between hypocrisy and diplomacy is thin. Who knows how many wars have been averted because someone said just the right thing? Faith might or might not move mountains, but flattery sure does.

The church lady (fifty-something) continues to barrage me with suggestions about scarves, hats and shoes. If I wore this or that I would look so much better. The other church lady (also fifty-something) behind the counter with her, nicely attired in designer wear, agrees.

The two may be right; still, my late husband made me feel I was good just as I was. He never told me I should change my look— straighten my hair, or straighten my back. He didn't even ask me to shave my legs. He had no need for embellishment or improvements. He loved me despite my flaws. He never asked anything of me except to cook dinner, and that I liked doing, so it wasn't a chore.

Examining some hand-knitted items on the counter, I tell my friend, the bachelorette: "I used to complain to my late husband that I didn't appreciate seeing his old shoes in the doorway and now I wish his shoes were right where he left them. There is no one to pester anymore; there are no mismatched pair of old shoes welcoming this homeowner with an inarticulate masculine odour, no husband willing to be reprimanded for keeping his footgear at hand. Back when I did have a husband who walked through the front door forever optimistic, expecting, I suppose, to be rewarded with a kiss, I often managed to ruin his entrance. 'Take off your shoes, I just washed the floor,' I'd say. Back then I had no idea that I should have behaved better. I always had something to complain about—starting from the mud on his shoes that he inadvertently brought in with the groceries he had purchased, and the fact that he often managed to miss an item or two from the list I had so carefully prepared for him. Back then I focused on his inability to carry out my wishes rather than the fact that he had tried to do it. How little did I know that there would come a time when I would not have a male servant to attend to my wishes. For if I am honest about it, I did often treat my husband as part butler, part chauffeur, part handyman, and worst of all, part mule. Who would have known that one day I would long for the unsavoury sight of old shoes by the doorway as they once held the beautiful feet of my husband? Beautiful? I never thought of his feet as beautiful when he was alive. Sometimes I think any man's shoes would be better to have around, than no shoes at all."

"So do you want to buy this scarf or not?" the church lady behind the counter asks, more interested in making a profit for Jesus, than loving her widowed neighbour as herself.

Do I want to buy her stuff? Not really. What I want is the stench of my husband's old shoes messing up my life again. That's what I want.

The other church lady, the one in designer wear, admits she too would like to pair up, but it's not that easy at "our" age. She tells me: "I have been divorced for seven years, and I have never been on a date. There are no men to go out with—they're either married or dating women half our age. The chances for women over 55 finding another partner are nil. It won't happen—you won't fall in love again. You are too old."

And I thought she would be more interested in raising funds for the church than giving Despair a chance.

"No one is ever too old to fall in love," my friend tells the divorcee, her voice raised.

When there is a sudden downpour of rain, you don't need the army to arrive in small boats to carry you to safety; all you need is an umbrella. When someone hurts your feelings, you don't need an army of do-gooders to come to your aid. One indispensable friend is all you need, and lucky for me, I have one.

# 34

Taking out the paprika container from the spice rack, preparing lunch for the Nemeth clan, I remember how my late husband loved the kitchen more than any other room in the house. Suddenly I am engulfed by pleasant memories of our shared cooking adventures: paprika potatoes, paprika chicken, goulash and stuffed cabbage, Hungarian style. Food contains good tidings; possibly that's why it plays such an important part in religious ceremonies. Hindus, who believe in reincarnation, offer food to their Gods in the hope their edible gifts will win them favour (if not in this life, then in the next). For Catholics, God is present in the consecrated Host which is distributed to the parishioners, who prefer it to coffee and donuts, as it contains the magical ingredient that will guarantee them life after death.

Is it time to turn off the oven? I check the clock and notice it's not working. It stopped at 11:50 a.m. The exact time of my husband's death.

"A coincidence," one son says.

"Stop being so superstitious," the other says. Yes but ... why shouldn't I imagine their father is here and about? I miss their father more than I can say. If all the cathedrals in the world were turned into condominiums for the rich, if suddenly only the rich could afford to travel to Europe, well I would miss these things, but not as much as I now miss their father.

That voice in my head tells me: "Widow Mary, you have to learn to be self-sufficient. Don't expect your children to help you bear your grief. That would be unfair."

That voice is right. And yet I can't help it—I need my sons' protection from the Dark Force. It is goading me to self-destruct. The fact that I own a house doesn't do much to stop the Dark Force in its tracks. The added bars on the basement windows also do nothing to protect me from It. The Dark Force seeps in through the cracks in my thoughts. It isn't my family doctor or the cute antics of my cat that can stop the Dark Force from making a quick dissolution into the St. Lawrence River appear attractive. What stops It is the fact my husband did not leave me alone—he left me with two sons.

Unconditional love is a child's birthright. A parent is in his debt. In his safekeeping: the next generation.

Ding dong. At the door—my step-children and their families.

"Can't we make grandpa all new again?" Aiden, my 4-year-old step grandson, asks.

It would be possible to live in a world without children, but it wouldn't be the world we have grown fond of. Children have the job of cheering up their elders, and do a fine job of it. Families thrive. The well-oiled machine is in working order.

"What's for lunch?" one son asks, and then another.

The real question to be answered right now is where do we eat—in the kitchen or in the dining room?

Personally I would rather eat out in the garden than in any kitchen or dining room. Even my best friend's newly-renovated gem of a kitchen or a seat in a top-rated restaurant doesn't appeal half as much as eating outside, amidst a host of flowers I myself planted and gave life to. (I ordered them to sneak out of the earth and bring forth mirth and good wishes and they did). But it's winter, so there is no garden to go to. In the summer the hanging baskets of flowers are a testament to my power as a witch; well, maybe not, maybe they're just a testament to my buying power. Still, I'm the one who put them up. They add a touch of class, but what of it? The snow-white landscape is just as pretty, though not as welcoming.

At the head of the dining room table, with my family around me, I'm at peace with how my life turned out. Generally, I'm not. Generally, I'm the lady with a chip on her shoulder, the ugly duckling, the failed writer of fables, but, with my family around me, there is no place for regret or self-pity.

Like the shell of a mollusc protects the critter inside it, humans also come into the world with a natural outer covering—first mothers shield newborns, and then everyone else chips in. Very little can break our spirit.

"What is the best advice your father ever gave you?" I ask the kids.

Common consensus: "You don't have to come first, just try not to be last."

He didn't push others to do well. Still, he came to Montreal, with nothing to his name, a Hungarian refugee from a repressive Communist regime, and in a few years succeeded in getting a Ph.D.

I tell the kids: "Once when I asked your father if he felt more Hungarian or Canadian, he said he was 'oscillating between the two worlds.' Is that what he is doing now, I wonder (oscillating between this world and the next)?"

No one round the dining room table has an answer, but Aiden, the four-year-old, wonders whether he can play with the cat? That's children for you—they remind you that you have to concentrate on how to play, and not how to suffer. Who is in the room with you is more important than who is missing.

The sound of a family when they are in tune with each other is like the sound a star makes when it is being born. That sound can't be heard, but you can imagine it—it's big and boisterous and important in the cosmic scheme of things. Being surrounded by close family members is rejuvenating. You feel yourself back in the womb of possibilities ...

After lunch, after the dishes have been washed and put away, after the kids have gone, nostalgic for my late husband's company, I take out a book of poems he penned for me. Once upon a time Jesus used his own body to propel himself into heaven; I use my late husband's love poems. Actually I am not so sure there is a heaven to get to, until I read them and then I am there. His love is the spaceship that gets me out of this world, and into his.

# LOVE POEMS FOR MY WIFE

by George Nemeth

## New Harbor, Block Island

The ships call on their home port.
It is the place where they get replenished;
receive a new coat of paint;
are refueled or have their sails mended.
You are therefore my home port
where I am outfitted with new sails;
where I have my bottom caulked;
where I lie in my familiar berth;
where the water swings me with a green rhythm
against a blue-silver mirror showing
me a favourable likeness; in simple words:
the bay of your love receives me
with the turquoise song of serenity.

***

## On Love

It is not in the heart where the unbounded(ed) passion begins or ends.
Nor is it in that organ we were once taught to be ashamed of,
or at least think uncomfortable thoughts when it swells so easily
to the touch of swift, squeezing fingers
or a quick-march of blatant images, the sun-licked skin,
of freshly washed hair and a voice, small, submissive, a corrupted
    schoolgirl;
Adler's adopted daughter who wins by losing.

Not even in the brain where endorphins bathe testosterone-primed
    cells—
oh, yes, the chemistry of love now stands as revelation,
but Passion's platinum doors stay bolted; the secret undisclosed,
the salty wave of desire falls rhythmically on the sands of inner time

on the metaphoric shore we ran so often with sandals in hand
while a few yards away curious dolphins played.

But desire is not a wave; water obeying the Moon's command;
*it passeth understanding* like God's peace in the last blessing of the Mass.
Nor are the nerves, the imperfect pathways through which we trace
the amplified messages of the midbrain willing to transliterate
the synaptic jump into that feeling that lasts and lasts
after the rocketry of lust exploded; the fall of multicoloured stars
into the void; the cliché-d image of fireworks under an inflammable sky
with real celestial bodies which somehow represent *your* body.

For this is about your body and mine.

It is *your* skin, *your* hair, *your* tongue, *your* voice from a wilderness—
that is your pubic hair. Little red, riding hooded:
the statue of St. Clit at the crossroads—and I kneel.
I bring the flower of my tongue to the saint. The tiny statue smiles.
And then the kiss. And then the wild ride of the ghost train
in the wet night of the Tunnel of Love complete with silky sound effects.

And the journey stops and starts—each time the track seems different—
each time the first time. The first and only time.
And this is how it is: First, the wish to touch and taste
Second, to have and hold
The Third, to control and possess
before I give myself up to you in turn,
that you may possess me utterly *world without end*
as we pause on those sands no hourglass can hold
and for a moment I forget that I am;
the armour of gilded consciousness has slid into the sea
and the bitter burden of self falls away
may death ever come in this form
angel

\*\*\*

## On a Photograph of Mary

As I look on this slice of reality forced into two dimensions
There are at first glance, objects, colours
beneath the glass of gloss, a set of memories
to stir when blander recollections fade behind the eyes.
On this one: Mary with basket,
basket with flowers, petals scattered on the grass,
gray brick wall to the left, tall bushes, trees behind her.
The image seems to say: here is The Gardener,
also the Chief Flower, the Prime Gift of this summer.
It is so recorded for all who may come after.
Look closer though: This picture embraces
a secret metaphor (revealed to me). *She herself is the Garden,*
*the garden of multicoloured delights; the blessed soil*
*from which life and these singular lives spring*
*inviting bees, butterflies to feast, humans to gaze*
*(maybe marvel and envy a bit)*
*at such a store of incontestable beauty.*
Now I understand the Great Romantics
who sang of Love and Beauty intertwined
in clear voices free and unashamed.
Against the formal floral orders of France and England
here grows a free, an unruly spirit,
a tiny peasant republic of liberated plants:
the rows of sparkling cups, of straw and velvet parasols,
slender stalks, Spring's green debutantes,
all this, and more: berries in midsummer,
sweet grapes at Summer's end and Fall is ushered in
with bouquets of aster.

Now, under winter's sheepskin coat
Everything sleeps. In dreams the hibernating roots
Whisper, awaiting next year's Resurrection:
*We are the Keepers. Mary's garden is Love.*
*Mary's garden is Mary.*

\*\*\*

I'm suddenly choked by a desire to write you a LETTER.
This letter should contain:
    1) a statement of love
    2) a statement of hope
    3) a statement of confusion as to why
1a) is this love so intense at times it prevents me from having a headache
1b) while at times it causes me to have one
1c) I am having an erection while I'm writing this
1d) at times I want to torture & mutilate you
1e) and mark your body with obscene wounds & hellish signs
1f) and kiss and lick your freshly forced body openings
    (viscosity of blood &V-8/vaginal juice)

2a) is there hope to have & hold your hand
    breasts smeared with semen
    buttocks
    feet

2b) do I hope for you to be with me as consort & comfort & fort
    (meaning strong)
    /and me in the stockade—imagine!
2c) will I hope to ward off death a step or two with your cheer, softness,
    head infinitesimally, bowed

2d  as my head is locked between your thighs—my ears block out
the screech of the
outer spheres

2e) I hope to lead you through the Fire & Water trials
(Tamino & Pamina: tricks & theatre
sounds and sights heroic
sweet tears, melodrama)

2f) I have hoped to use your arched body as a bridge to the the
undefined Left Bank
I'm halfway through—don't let your
belly button sag: heavenly trapdoor
how I would fall among your bowels
of horror and bladder of gall & gallantry

2g) I will have hoped for not refusing me in eternity
for our doings are limited by the biological
stopwatch
and the aforementioned death is an alternate guest at our feasts
& rollover
smiling politely a bony smile


3b) You must help me in my confusion

3c) or else confuse me more (a haze of lust of smoke rising from
embarrassed embers)

3d) for I want to be wrapped in the confusion of your tangled
thick hair

3e) and in the blanket of your pride and passion

3f) staring at the reddening horizon

3g) not knowing sunrise from sunset

3h) and not really caring anyhow.


\*\*\*

## A Short Poem of Love

*What are you writing?* A poem. *What kind?* A love poem.
*For whom?* For you. Mary leans toward my face.
*The girl the poem addresses is a* **chimera.**
*The body you touch with trembling hands*
*When evening comes does not really exist.*
*The odor of my skin (that stirs you)*
*Disperses in the quiet autumn air.*
*My oft praised brown eyes' glances*
*Dissolve in the blue haze of the afternoon.*
*And as in bad horror movies, your eager arms*
*Embracing my slim waist hold on to thin air.*
*My shy smile also disappears like an indifferent shadow.*
**I am like that.** *You see? Is this you love? Still? And why?*

You exist among your lively flowers. Among your brainy books.
You exist beside me, in the morning, at noon and in the night.
We eat lunch together. Spirits don't partake human food.
As you step into the bath
The smell of sunshine sings on your radiant skin.

How could I *not* love you? If this is fantasy,
What is the (so often chided) reality?

\*\*\*

## Twenty-Five Lines for Mary

Anchor. The metaphoric steadfast ship rides out the storm.
Becoming: a change, there is now what was not there before.
Create, announce us with a wild welcoming song
Depend on what we built; a fond foundation
Entrust to each other this secret emerald, this covenant

For now, and after this generation dissolves into ashes
Guard what is for us precious, peerless, perfect. Always
Homeward, as the angel looks in the purple twilight
Improvising on the twenty-five string harp. The pearly sounds
Jubilate above us. Crown and sceptre incline.
Keep this radiant kiss, the memento of this day of blossoms,
Love as in love as in lovely, as the exquisite
Mary meanders as a morning brook in the garden,
Nodding to the tulips, bowing to the daffodils, bending
 to the tiny violets
Oblivious to the swift sharp showers, to the noises of the city-machine.
Present in my embrace that catches the quills of the porcupine world.
Quiet as the summer sunset above Grand Boulevard
Retain, reward, re-form this intimate Council of Two,
Send this message to the hosts of the inner and outer universe:
Tomorrow this union will still stand and deliver
Under these Northern skies, under the ripening age and ages.
Victory, always victory as we touch, again and anew
Walk as we've mounted the twenty-five marble steps,
X-ray eyes may follow us, but we have nothing to hide:
You keep at my side. It is safe there. We'll move at a steady pace.

* * *

## A Valentine Poem

My Valentine is not funny.
She's gently serious, even sad at times
And flashes of anger are also not alien to her.
Her lips are kissable though and the years,
(those strange make-up artists) have been kind and attentive to her skin,
her voice, her graceful walk, her warm brown eyes,
her curly hair (that even strangers find seductive)
and this, my Valentine, is mine. Forever, I hope,

as the great red hearts are superimposed on the shadows of Time,
the great enemy (or friendly wizard)—as one chooses to perceive it
but You, my Valentine who wears her heart on her sleeve,
embrace me—on this particular day
and each following day, as they are all particular for you and me.

\* \* \*

## Part of a poem that might have been even longer ...

... Nevertheless the winter light
plays one-leg hopscotch on the ice
bird-stones cry their pond of tears
stretches taut below the surface (glossy)
it is funny it is frozen
it is guarded by silent pikes
it's surrounded by crucified roots
prophets martyrs would-be lovers ... (understudies ...)

You glide beyond the Earth's orange skin
to fall off pathetic skaters of Bosch (Jerome)
one reaches out with a handsome white net (Nabokov)
and behold there whirl the acrobatic butterflies turning upon
        themselves
in the coloured smokescreen of twisters of self-destruct dust.
One is transformed in free fall
one is transformed in the fall of captivity
but shall we (should we) be raised
incorruptible?

In your hands there sprouts a bouquet of mercy
among your toes the rose of miracle
your mouth bites with the bitterness of myrrh
and your body

arches taut as a rainbow
between two blue-black pot-bellied storms
against a Canadian evening ...

\*\*\*

## Serenade

It is now morning. I'm hanging out of this verse
like Peter Pan dangles at the edge of a cartoon
which is brought to your colour screen courtesy of
Fantastic Foods Limited (unlimited?)

It is now morning. I'm my own footprints in the sky:
Puss 'n Boots; stepping with that seven-league reach
the riches of the earth lie between my legs
the measure of continents the lay of the seven seas

It is now morning. I'm swept under the rock
under the volcano even. I reverberate
between the fast sweating black-sliver walls
my voice, my voices carry me. Carry me home.

It is now morning. It surprises me being alive
slightly off center but still in the universe
I miss you, Gulliver's wife, (Sinbad's?),
I miss you right in my bed, mistress of my silver-black sails.

# Spring Is Here

# WHAT IS IT
# YOU REALLY WANT?

## Year Ten

# 36

Happiness is …?
Crocuses ganging up against the snowy wall.
Happiness is …?

The first iris of the season: in each of its three petals (a holy trinity): good tidings. Flowers are superstars. And I'm a groupie—part of their ever-increasing fan base.

Spring tortures no one, but waiting for spring is a real test of endurance. Spring uproots winter's mechanical brain and implants something akin to bright feelings. Spring forces the earth to be receptive to growth. Spring forces women to be receptive to thoughts of newborns pushing tentacles into their careers. An urge to eat chocolate can't be compared to an urge to eat springtime—like comparing hunger to starvation. Spring pulls tulips out of the earth as if they were knots in a young girl's hair that have to come out. Spring inspires squadrons of newlyweds to demand good health and a house all paid for (heaven via express). Spring creates tempests in the hearts of old people—they're so wild they will knock off a cop (old age). Spring is a revolutionary. Spring arranged that all those who die confiscate something of importance …

Turn to the mirror expecting to have a nice day and you'll be disappointed. Best to turn to your backyard and get cracking.

Happiness is …? The first bouquet of the season: two yellow crocuses, one miniature blue iris and one snowdrop. Living art. Uncensored.

And then the snow hits. Snowflakes: shoeshine boys? Snowdrops: wipes …?

Minus 12 degrees centigrade. Unseasonably cold temperatures. I rush back in. Putting on my coat and boots I feel like a five-star general putting on her gear, before an important battle. And then I venture back out. Every snowflake, a bullet; every gust of wind, a machine gun—fire, set, go. The city is under siege and I am on the field, a general, inspecting the damage.

Most of the floral troops are still in their underground bunkers, polishing their boots, but the crocuses stand at attention and salute. The snow does them no harm; it actually protects them. They're a resilient bunch.

I turn to God, the Commander-in-Chief, as a soldier would turn to his superior, without thought, resentment or anger. God shovels Light my way. My faith in Christian principles is restored. Share the warmth.

Christopher Columbus stumbled upon America and made history. Discovering an unexpected bunch of yellow irises, snowdrops and crocuses near the garden gate, I think to myself: "A map of the world will do you no good; on the other hand, mapping out your garden will do you a world of good."

Happiness is ... A dramatic change in temperature.

Happiness is ... Spring riding on sunbeams; it offers first class tickets to good feelings. In my backyard I am the set designer, the stage hand, and the theatre director; the flowers are the stars of the show; they're ready to act in the classic drama: "Four Seasons." They don't need an audience to strut their stuff. Nor do they need applause. Is there is a lesson here (do likewise, and be content)?

I am this Morning's caretaker. Do no harm.

Early flowering tulips are status symbols. The first to come up and show off their good looks are noticed and admired. This year I am the first on my block to have them fly out of the earth and into my arms. Last year, in the backyard, they didn't do well, but transplanted to the front, they are thriving.

That voice in my head (is it the late Dr. George Nemeth?) tells me: "Individuals are not much different than flowers—where they're stationed affects their well-being. A child who doesn't do well in one school can blossom in another. The point is if you don't like your job, or your partner, do something about it. Make changes and be changed."

That voice in my head seems to have an opinion on everything. The real Dr. Nemeth was more prone to tell jokes than he was to hand out advice. If anything he might have told me: "The dead make good roommates—they don't take up space, they don't make noise, and they'll tell you what you want to hear! The downside is that they don't help with the rent."

My next door neighbour can't tell me if my late husband was more of a joker than a therapist but she can tell me (and she does) that last year he pruned the bushes near her fence, and this year, the bushes are overgrown, and her flowers are suffering for it.

"Chop down a tree," she says. "You have five." And then her doggie barks, and off she goes to do his bidding. If only my late husband's voice were as audible as this little animal's, but no such luck. All I have are recordings, memories ...

In mid-April, when the snow was still on the ground, my late husband would inevitably rush out and look in and around the water-logged trees, on the lookout for wood violets, and if he found a single specimen of the glorious spring flowers he would be as excited as a reporter getting the scoop of the year. He would cry out: "The wood violets are out," and then he would pick a whole bunch for me, his queen and consort.

Finding a clump of wood violets near the doorway, I drink in their scent. Like taking in that first cup of coffee of the day, the scent inspires confidence. Wood violets are scented invitations to a gala event. You don't have to be rich or famous to get one; you don't even have to know how to read to get the message: "God loves thee, girl!"

Wood violets are tiny floral specimens; it requires a great deal of patience to pick them. My husband had it, but I don't. I was happy and now I'm not.

That in-the-skull therapist has an opinion. "If contemplating a wee flower could cure the blues, psychologists would be out of business. And capitalism would come to an abrupt halt—no more spending sprees. When you're down, really down, flowers don't do a thing to cheer you up; what you need is someone to love you. How old you are is dependent on how many times you are told: 'I love you.' Each 'I love you' makes you younger by a day or a week or a year, whatever is required."

All very well but the one who used to tell me, "I love you," over and over again, isn't here, and I miss him. I miss that man like a chair might miss one of its legs if a chair had feelings. I miss him as much as I might miss having a chair if the courts impounded all my worldly possessions.

The history of the universe began when God decided to share Him/Herself with the material world. Where would the universe be without God? Without its history? Wouldn't it still be struggling to be born? So too would I be struggling to be who I am were it not for my dear old husband. My history began the day he decided to love me. Now that's a big jump—from Day 1 of the known universe to Day 1 of this Mary-being—and yet I dare to compare the two.

That in-the-skull therapist has an opinion. "Everyone starts life wanting to be loved, and everyone ends their life wanting to be loved; it's a never-ending story. You can fall in love once, twice, three times. You can love at twenty, thirty, or eighty. There is no time limit."

The thought of the day: The universe is an open book, divinely inspired. Read between the lines and discover it's a love story with a surprise ending.

# 37

"What is it you really want?" my friend, the bachelorette, asks, while the two of us look around for hanging plants at the Jean-Talon outdoor market.

"I want a man in my life."

"Who doesn't," she says.

Yes, but she has been single all her life, she can handle it, I can't. Damn it I need a man in my life as much as a woman who lost her house in a fire needs a roof over her head—it's that simple a thing. There it is—I am thinking less and less that I want my husband back, and more and more that I want a man in my life.

"At times I don't even remember what my late husband looked like," I tell my friend, confessing that I am starting to forget the late Dr. George Nemeth like one forgets a flock of birds that pass by; one notes the V pattern and is awed, and then just as quickly expects to be awed by another spectacular show of strength from Mother Nature.

"I've been in and out of relationships for years," she tells me, admiring a fabulous arrangement of multi-coloured geraniums. And adding something to the effect that of late, she thinks of the TV as her live-in-companion. And as for sex, well, use your imagination.

In days gone by when my husband ministered to my body, I was one of the luckiest ladies on the planet, I tell her. Now without my husband loving it, I feel like I am trapped inside someone else's body. Comedies have been made where just such a thing happens, but I can't think of anything funny in my own situation.

"The fact is older men prefer younger broads," my friend tells me. "They will try their darndest to pick up young chicks, and nine out of ten times, succeed; for older gals the reverse is true. Nobody wants them. Just think—an antique portrait of a young woman will fetch more than one by the same artist of an older woman."

"That's depressing," I say wishing she had kept the information about antique portraits to herself.

"Older women know better than to waste their time at bars where they have a hard time picking up men," she says. "So they do the next best thing—they go to their gardens and pick substitutes. Actually those-in-the-know know garden-variety dildos are not up to par; the made-in-China plastic variety are much more reliable, if you get my meaning."

My comrade-in-arms avoids one-night-stands; she prefers floral conquests, living art, to men who would rather be pleasured, than give pleasure. She used to buy sex toys aplenty, and now here she is buying garden shears.

So there it is—mirrors conspire against women; flowers come to their rescue. Any man can make a woman regret having loved him, but no flower will do it.

My friend tells me: "It takes more energy to beef up an older man's pride, help him blossom, than it does to make things come up in the garden, if you get my meaning."

"I get it alright," I tell her, "but is it the right attitude? A young woman assumes she's doing an older man a favour when she allows him the use of her pretty body; a young man also assumes the same thing when he offers himself to an older woman. But unlike their male counterparts, old crones are generally less diplomatic; they correct their sexual partners' mistakes. An error in judgement. Charity plays a big part in the bedroom. Pretence is an essential tool in the art of living and liking it. And in the art of fucking."

"Mary, what would you know? You only slept with one man— your late husband."

"That's true," I admit. My late husband took care of my body as a paediatrician takes care of his tiny tots—he made sure I was in good health. A massage therapist works over a movie star's body (a lot is invested in the top notch young starlet) so did my husband do the same. He ministered to my body, and now, without him, I am at a loss. A maiden-in-distress. SOS. What to do?

"Let's go to Italy," my friend says.

"I don't have that kind of money."

"Spend less on your garden, and you might have."

"I shouldn't over-spend on gardening supplies, but I do it anyway."

Like food or wine connoisseurs, garden aficionados can go over-board. There is something comic, downright foolish, in being consumed by any one thing. When you come right down to it, what is being created that is truly original in a garden? You might think 'your' flowers don't have that run-of-the mill look that everyone else's flowers do, but whom are you kidding? Still, how pretty your garden grows is in direct proportion to your income and, if your income is low (my income is low), well, you just have to stretch that dollar, and make it work for you.

I tell my friend: "Choosing a hanging plant is kind of like going to a whorehouse: you look around, and say: 'That's the one.' Some hanging plants age gracefully, and some do a miserable job of it. Often, the ones which are the prettiest at the start of the season are the very ones which will fail to keep up their good looks. The same goes for women. The prettiest in high school are not necessarily the ones who look best when they're older; you need hardy plants, just as you need hardy girls to look great at fifty. The hardier hanging plants often don't make a good first impression, but they'll give you the best bang for your buck. Come September they'll still be around, decorating your front porch, while the dainty little things put out in early May will have dropped out of sight. To know what plants to buy you need experience. Age."

"The older we get, the wiser we are and that's useful in a garden, but in the bedroom—it backfires," she says. "Men of any age prefer youth—innocence. Ignorance. It's not fair. Getting old terrifies the shit out of me."

"As someone once said (was it Oscar Wilde?): 'Don't be afraid of old age. It doesn't last long.'"

My friend, the confirmed bachelorette, a grand dame, takes out her make-up kit, and re-touches her lips. "When I was twenty," she says, eyeing herself rather critically in the mirror, "I used to put up my hems—I always wore my skirts above the knee, whatever the current style—but then I hit fifty, and I started to put the hems down, but that's easier said than done. (Often there isn't enough material to work with.) My legs are nice enough, but they don't match my face, meaning I'm too old to be a sex object, and too young to be a corpse. What to do? How to dress? Mini-skirts invite attention; suits deflect it. If a woman has lots of eggs in her basket, she should advertise it, but if she doesn't, it's best to lie low and wear a Chanel suit. There is nothing attractive about getting older, though most of us imagine we look good for our age. Even if we didn't, it wouldn't register. Our brain lies to us. It tells us we're still in our 30s when we're anything but."

I agree. No one thinks of themselves as being old—it's part of our Cavewoman's Survival Kit. That's why younger gals are used to sell anything from dentures to disposable underwear.

Mother Nature owns a chain of beauty salons which caters to a select clientele—the under-thirty crowd. Her customers walk in looking great, and come out looking even greater. In an ideal world Mother Nature (or is it Father Nature?) would be brought to court for age discrimination; in the real world the over-thirty crowd can't do a bloody thing.

That voice in my head has an opinion and it is this: "Anything is better than whining about Mother Nature, the bitch. Turn to the mirror carrying a grudge and it will appear cracked. Past fifty, one would hope that a woman has outgrown her childish desire to be a beauty. A woman ought to apply herself to loftier goals—start a business, do volunteer work, or garden, for heaven's sake. Miss America pageant winners are awarded a potpourri of prizes, including a year's supply of perfume. But any woman, of any age, can go into a garden and get her fill of fragrances. In a garden everyone, young or old, can win first prize. (You're perfect—as is!) Why should you compare yourself to a rose when you can compare yourself to a tree? At a nursery young trees can be had for next to nothing. A mature tree costs an arm and a leg. Also, the ocean is old and wrinkled, but does it detract from its value? Beauty comes in all shapes & sizes & ages. Turn to the mirror hoping for a miracle (how young you look!) and you'll be disappointed; turn to the mirror believing anyone born of a woman is a miracle in the making and you can't but feel good."

The thought of the day: Turn to the mirror as if it were your neighbor's backyard. Accept what you cannot change.

Another thought: Turn to the mirror as if it were a cockroach, and you an exterminator, and you'll live to tell the tale.

# 38

The wind wraps itself round me like a warm scarf. It's nice, but it's not nice enough. I want what I had—a partner. The question is: Would my late husband approve?

"Of course, he would approve," Josie, a popular Montreal travel agent and friend, says.

"My late husband was possessive. He would have put up with anything, except infidelity. If I had strayed, he would have tossed me out."

"But you didn't stray. You had it good."

"I did have it good, but now here I am dreaming of being part of a couple again, dreaming of sharing breakfasts and lunches and dinners and midnight snacks with a significant other. Can I, should I, dare I think I can have a second chance at love?"

"Of course, you should," Josie says. "Those who pass on to the Other Side want those they left behind to be happy."

"I suppose."

"When my mother died I sensed she was still around, looking out for me. I often ask for her help."

"I ask my late husband for help as well."

The Catholic Church teaches us to pray for the dead, but most of us pray to the dead. It seems as soon as someone we love passes away we turn them into saints whose favours we court. I didn't expect it to happen to me, but it did. My late husband was far from perfect—when he died he had debts which I was saddled with, but none of that matters now. Everything is forgiven.

Death is the ultimate living eraser, erasing all the bad deeds, the bad arguments, the ridiculous putdowns and countless faux pas; what remains is the divine spark inside that gorgeous individual that was, and is no more.

Often, I make a bouquet and turn my kitchen (George's favourite place) into a little shrine. I pray for good health and the courage to offer those who need my love, love, and failing that, charity ... Jesus wants us to be good, but I can't be good unless I have a man sharing my bed. My soul is at risk here—if I don't find someone to help me get rid of the garbage of lust, I'll ... I don't know what I will do, but whatever it is, Jesus would not be pleased.

"Mary, you were loved. That knowledge will give you the confidence that you will need to look for another partner," my friend tells me.

She might be right. My husband did not leave me defenceless—I am armed—armed with his insistence that I was an "indescribable beauty" (his opinion, not mine), armed with his good wishes (only the best for his Mary), armed with his self-confidence (he thought I could do anything I set my mind to!), armed with his I-love-yous—I should be able to take on the dating world, and hope to come out ahead. But can I?

I ask Josie: "How can I be 100 per cent certain my husband is OK with my looking for a partner, when I myself, I am NOT OK with him being with someone else?"

"My cousin, Phil, is a medium. Ask him."

"I don't believe in any of that hocus pocus stuff. Mediums are scam artists."

"Some are, but my cousin is the real deal. When he was a little boy, he saw the spirits of our dead relatives. He spoke to them."

The Catholic Church doesn't approve of seeking mediums out for a consult, and I can't say I do either. But this is not any old medium out to make a buck (his fees are minimal); this is my friend's cousin. The two grew up together in the same neighbourhood. He might, just might, be able to provide some clues as to what my late husband is a-thinking.

Let the talks begin ...

Phil takes a brief look at a photo of my late husband and says: "The man in the photo is a joker."

That he was.

"Your husband—George—is telling me that you changed the furniture around in the bedroom."

That I did, but then who doesn't do that kind of thing? Mediums simply mirror what you tell them—they pick up information and instantly relay it back to you. Mediums, like mirrors, use low-tech wizardry to succeed in impressing their clients.

Phil pauses for a moment, and then says: "George is asking me to ask you where did you put the Hungarian carpet that was hanging on the bedroom wall?"

"In the basement," I answer, wondering how Phil could possibly have known that I had taken down the carpet from the wall. Most mediums stick to generalities, but this is a detail Phil (or Josie) couldn't possibly have known.

"This is odd," Phil says. "I see George jumping on the bed. Why would he do that?"

"He liked to jump up and down for no reason. It used to embarrass our kids to no end ... Ask him if he approves of my looking for a new partner?"

"George is telling me to tell you that it was good that you loved him, but now someone else needs your love."

Someone else needs my love ...? Can it be true ...? Am I being told by my late husband that I should seek this someone out? Is it possible?

Phil raises his hand, and says: "Wait. There is another message but it doesn't make any sense to me whatsoever. George is saying and I quote: 'You will be he.'"

"I will be he?"

And then Phil says: "I can't do this anymore."

"This is it?"

"It's not up to me," he says. "The spirits don't linger."

He escorts me to the door.

"How did it go?" Josie asks.

"Your cousin said what I wanted to hear," I tell her, unconvinced a nondescript-looking 40-something, who sold used cars for a living, and whose little office was tucked in the basement of his little house in a Montreal suburb, could possibly be able to break down the insurmountable barriers between this world and the next.

"Phil is a good man," Josie says. "He bears no ill-intentions."

"The impulse to help the bereaved can be so overwhelming that people will sometimes go to any length to do it."

"That's possible," she says. "There is no shame in wanting to help, or in asking for help and accepting it."

"There is no shame in looking for someone to love, but I can't see myself doing it."

"Try."

"It's not fair," I say to Josie. "George was in his forties when I met him and I was in my twenties. May-September romances don't work. The younger one gets short-shifted."

Love and lust might guarantee a till-death-do-you-part, but it can't guarantee a happily-ever-after. Someone leaves first.

"Are you blaming George for dying or for loving you?" my friend asks.

"The answer is I blame myself—I can't make it on my own. I need help navigating through life."

"Everyone does."

That in-the-skull therapist agrees. "Most of us come into the world badly put together; our parents ought to repair the damage, but parents often fail miserably in their attempt to fix what is broken. Only a partner's love can repair the damage. Those who find it are the lucky ones."

Don't I know it—love fills up the empty spaces in your life with life-giving properties—oxygen on-the-go. And yet love can also be ferocious. Like a pack of wild dogs on the loose, love can tear apart those who would do you harm. Love offers the best personal security system available. It protects you from bullies and thieves who are out to steal your self-worth; it also defends you against self-hate. It tells you over and over again that you are right just the way you are. I had such love, and now I don't.

Thought of the day: No one can be 100 per cent sure what those in the Otherworld are thinking, but Jesus did say that in heaven people neither marry nor are given in marriage, but will be like angels (Matthew 22:30). And that's why it's quite OK for widows to look for a new partner.

Another thought: Flowers and the rise and the set of the sun can be magical, but Love contains the miraculous.

Spring Courses

# WHAT IS YOUR PASSION?

Year Ten

# 39

Hunting for a mate is a dangerous occupation—do it and you risk getting hurt. If you are well-armed (youth helps), you have a chance at capturing the prey (marital bliss); unarmed, watch out! If only I could equate hunting for a mate with fox hunting—a game fit for the royal family. Unfortunately, I identify with the animals on the run, rather than with the ladies in their designer riding gear.

My friend, Olga, the divorcee, reminds me that one in five couples meet on on-line dating sites.

"Give it a try," she says, ready and willing to give me a tutorial on how to use Plenty-of-Fish, a free on-line dating service. When it comes to dating on-line, it's not necessarily the fittest that survive, but the luckiest.

"OK, let's do it," I say.

"Not so fast," she says, indicating that you have to do three things before you can put yourself "out there." First, you have to take a good photograph. (It can't be too flattering, or the fellows will be disappointed when they meet you in person.). Second, you have to re-christen yourself. (You can't use your real name.) And third, you have to compose a dating profile. Show-and-Tell. In theory the information you put on the dating site is supposed to give clues to who you are. (What makes you unique!) But in fact, it's an ad, promising the moon.

"What is your passion?" she asks.

I can't think of anything. Travel? No. Short of funds. Rough it out in the woods? And be lost there? No, thank you. Ballroom dancing? Not with this left footer!

"Dinner & a movie—that's me," I tell my friend.

"You have to avoid clichés. Stand out from the crowd."

"Like I'm an Olympic champion skier? Or a world-famous soprano? Stand-up comic? I am none of these things."

At least an older man can use money as bait and sweet young things will eat it up, but older women can throw their money around and still not get the catch of the day.

Olga tells me: "You can always stretch the truth—a little. Men generally overstate their height by two inches, and women, understate their age and weight."

Coming up with an on-line dating profile is as much fun as preparing for college entrance exams. I don't want to do it.

I tell my friend: "They say men only want women past the big five-oh for one of two things: *purse* or *nurse*."

"That's true. There are men who prey on older women—they are more interested in getting into their bank accounts than into their pants."

And I thought she would beef up my courage, and here she is scaring me to death. I can put bars on my windows, extra locks on my doors, but then I can meet a guy and say: "Come on in," and before I know it my life savings are wiped out.

When I was married to my dear old husband, I didn't have to worry about anything. I could look like a slob; I could be whiny, bitchy, needy, and still be loved. That man was ready for sex any-time, anywhere. Now, as a single woman, I am expected to have my nails manicured, my feet pedicured, and I better go to the gym and pump iron. ('Cause the arms jiggle, and it's no dance jiggle.)

What to do …? Adapt to being single. Hermits go off and live in the desert for years and they manage to thrive on self-deprivation. Maybe I could too.

That in-the-skull therapist has an opinion. "You don't have to resign yourself to being single. If it's cold you don't resign yourself to staying in. You put on a coat, and get on with your day. You do what you have to do."

If only I could …

"My neighbour found her husband on-line and she's no spring chicken," my friend tells me.

Yes, there is hope (or is there?) ... Hunting for a mate is like going to your garden expecting to find a patch of wild strawberries. Just because your friend in another part of the city was lucky to have found the plant spreading its beautiful tentacles round the iron fence separating her property from the rest of the world is no reason why you should as well. I vaguely recall that my late husband once found a couple of ripe strawberries next to our maple tree and offered them to me. He recognized which plants were edible and which weren't long before they flowered; I, on the other hand, couldn't. So here I am dreaming about enticing a man out of his cave and into mine, and all I can think of is the one who was successfully hunted down by cancer.

My body longs for a man's attention, but not any man's. A polar bear coming out of hibernation instinctively longs for fresh fish and seeks out their habitat, eager to re-establish himself. I too am in need of sustenance, and it's not spirit food I want to feast on. God how I miss having regular married ladies' sex! Other widows might miss travelling with their husbands to Europe or exotic lands; as my husband and I didn't do that, I can't really miss it. What I miss the most is my late husband's tongue travelling between my legs. This is the area of the world (my world) I would like him to visit but this will not happen. Other widows might miss playing cards or board games with their dear old husbands; not me, we never played those games. The only game I miss is having sex with my late husband. I often find myself imagining I am in the act of copulation with the man who loved me above all others. I can tell people I miss his love, but I can't admit I want to have sex with that late husband of mine. If I did, I would be as welcome as a paedophile. You can admit to masturbating, but if you admit wanting sex with a dead man, then they might lock you up in a loony bin.

"Don't wallow in self-pity," my friend says, checking out the photos of the over-fifty crowd posted on Plenty-of-Fish. There are a number of men to pick from—a retired engineer, a graphic designer and a salesman—any one of them could provide carnal pleasure. (But do I want them? Not really.)

Being in a police station and going through their photo files to identify a crook might be less spooky than checking out what's available on a dating site. The rate of sexually transmitted diseases (STDs) is increasing in leaps and bounds in the over-fifty crowd—everyone knows it. Even AIDS is a threat.

For over three decades I had a husband who protected me from bad men—men who would hurt me. I was courted, lusted after and adored. Why I should have been chosen to be the love of his life is hard to figure out. I can't even drive or swim! Still, he took me in. When he was around I had the illusion there were no bad guys, no thieves, no rapists lurking in the shadows. He was more than a bodyguard. He was an entire police force hired to protect me.

How can I go on a blind date? I don't even have the courage to look at myself in the mirror. I avoid mirrors like cowards avoid confrontations. Everything takes longer, except getting older.

Someone says (is it the late Dr. George Nemeth?): "Turn to the mirror as if it were a vase and you, the water, and soon enough someone will want to make use of what you have."

True or false: Flowers come in every shade except grey?

Thought of the day: Turn to the mirror as if it were a cigarette lighter and you a chain smoker—you'll not find an aging bombshell, but a bomb in the making. Meaning? Grey power = flower power??

Mellow yellow. Humans turned wolves into dogs, tigers into cats. Flowers took pity and turned an ugly world into a pretty one. Bark once if you agree; twice, if you don't.

# 40

Fast and furious. For $200,000 you can hitch a ride in a Russian-made space shuttle and go around the world in 92 minutes; for the price of a cup of coffee you can have your heart broken in record time—10 seconds. Internet dating sites make it possible to meet X number of blind dates for X number of times and remain unattached. Speed is the thing. For adventurers meeting face-to-face with those that they are introduced to on-line, the experience invokes pleasure. For those who dread anything that is new and daring (take me!), well, they should look elsewhere for comfort, because dating is not for sissies.

Advice columnists suggest that, when you meet an individual you have been introduced to on-line, you should: a) Do so during the day and in a public place; b) Let a friend know where you are; c) Avoid disclosing your family name or phone number, and d) Don't accept a ride home. And one more thing—you better bring along a sense of humour; that's vital. Without one, you might lose your marbles. (If you haven't lost them already.) And remember the first meeting with someone you clicked with on-line is called a 'coffee interview'—it's not a date! So go ahead—have fun with it.

Meeting an individual you have been matched with on a dating site is as much fun as crossing a busy highway. There are no traffic lights and no policemen to guide you … What to wear? A padded bra or unpadded one? Dark red lipstick or lip gloss? If you're over 50 you definitely don't want to appear frumpy, but if you try too hard to look sexy you might unwittingly be mistaken for a man in drag. (What a drag that would be!) What's age appropriate? High heels? Pumps? The last time I was on a blind date I was 20 years old and had chestnut brown hair down to my waist …

But now here I am taking the risk and I am scared to death.

I step into the café; the interviewee, a 70-year-old retired English teacher and amateur musician, meets me at the door with a rose.

(How nice!) The man appears more nervous than I am. (How nice!) Accidently spilling his coffee, he apologizes profusely, and goes on to tell me the details of his life: He was never married, never sired any children, though he did live common law for eight years with a beautiful and brilliant East European woman. I like this man. I give him my phone number and my email.

And then somehow the subject of sex comes up and I admit I enjoy a roll in the hay. (Or something like that.)

"This is going way too fast for me," the fellow says.

Before I know it the interview is over; the man escorts me to the door with the promise that he would call me ...

Days go by—no call.

Like a child who falls down and is surprised by the pain, I am taken aback—how can this be? Why does it hurt so much? This man whom I met was supposed to like me (I liked him) and he was supposed to call me and then the two of us would go out and see a movie, and then, the whole shebang.

All my friends say the same thing: "Move on."

It's not that simple. Like a child who has just been told there is no Santa Claus I feel betrayed. It's not supposed to be like this.

A friend says: "You shouldn't have brought up the subject of sex. Older men can't get it up. They just want someone to hold hands with. Go for younger men."

I don't want to go for anyone—this is a hell of a game, and I don't want to play it ... And then it hits me—I know an entire army of divorcees, bachelorettes and long-standing un-merry widows who have been looking for a partner and failed in their attempts. Why did I think I could succeed? I guess I had been so spoiled by my late husband's unconditional love that I assumed, the fool that I was, that it would be as easy as pie to find a match.

Being single is no fun at all. I miss my husband. Like a nun longs for her prayer book when it is not within her grasp, I long for my husband's company. No, it's worse than that—I long for him like a nun would long for her profession if suddenly the Pope decided there will be "No More Nuns!" The Pope will never say: "No More Nuns." But God has said No to me: "You'll never see your husband again."

Sorrow is a slow poison. Just when you think you are free of it, it resurfaces. The planet Earth is set to destruct in a few billion years; my husband's death sent me off into the future. Propelled to the end of time, I find myself in an airless environment. I can't breathe.

Calling Dr. Nemeth. It seems he's not in ... Better call the medical clinic for psychiatric help. And I do that ... Sorry all the staff is booked for the next six months. What to do? Book an appointment with a private therapist and pay through the nose?

If I recall correctly my late husband didn't think talk therapy was all that effective. On the other hand he was a strong advocate of self-help groups. If someone came to him with an alcohol addiction problem, he would refuse them treatment unless they agreed to attend AA meetings. That was a prerequisite. He also recommended Recovery International, a self-help group, which uses a system of cognitive behavioural techniques which can provide relief for anger, depression, anxiety, stress and insomnia.

I look up Recovery International on the internet and find that members of this program, based on the ground-breaking work of the late Dr. Abraham Low, meet once a week. In between the group members can help themselves by recalling maxims (or spots) such as a) "Discomfort can be patiently borne, bravely faced and humbly tolerated," b) "Mistakes are a healthy and valuable part of life" and c) "Choose hope rather than gloom, doom and despair."

The advice on the internet site is very good; it sets me answering the questions posed:

"Do you have the will to courage?"

"Yes," I decide.

"Do you have the will to treat mental health as a business and not as a game?"

I suppose.

"Do you have the will to take yourself less seriously?"

I hope so.

"Do you realize humour is your best friend, temper, your worst enemy?"

Definitely.

"Do you have the courage to make a mistake?"

Sometimes.

"Lower your expectations and your performance will rise."

All I know is that I don't know.

"Can you do the things you fear and hate to do?"

Probably not.

"Endorse yourself for the effort, not the performance."

I can do that.

"Every day is full of frustration and disappointment."

That it is.

"You don't need to be saint, hero or angel."

And what if I am rotten to the core?

"Wear the mask."

And if I can't?

"Try, fail, try fail; try, succeed."

If only I could.

# 41

I long for what I had (marital bliss) but what of it?—the laundry needs to be done; the dishes need to be washed. Actually, the real problem is that, no matter how much soap I use, I can't get the depressing stains out of my thoughts.

That in-the-skull therapist tells me: "Look up at the sky and be grateful you don't have to clean it. Someone else does the work. Mother Nature is a top-notch cleaning lady. There, in the garden, surrounded by all that dirt, flowers manage to stay clean and fresh. Trees are vacuum cleaners and air purifiers—two in one. Engineers should turn to Mother Nature for direction, and mimic her."

It's cold and the weathergirl says it might snow, but what of it? I rush to the garden—no hat, no gloves. A real nut case. The cold: a veritable straitjacket.

Planting annuals in my front yard cheers me up. The more I plant, the less I want to go down to the basement and do the laundry. If I lack the sky, I lack joy. If I lack joy, I lack direction.

A neighbour and his wife pass by. The man looks at my boxes of annuals and tells me: "It's too early in the season to plant annuals. You should plant them on a cloudy, fairly warm day when they will suffer the least shock."

"I couldn't help myself," I tell him. Don't I know it?—planting annuals too early is akin to having unprotected sex. I should have just said, No, but I was so eager to get my floral babies up and coming, that I caved in.

"You have a lovely perennial garden," I tell my neighbour. "What's your secret?"

"Topsoil, peat moss and fertilizer. I add some every year."

I think to myself: Spending money on topsoil is like buying underwear—the more disposable income you have, the higher the quality of what you hide down below.

My neighbour must have guessed what I was thinking because soon enough he gives me a lecture on how to turn biodegradable kitchen waste into top-grade fertilizer. His knowledge is formidable and I'm impressed. In my youth I revered professors who professed that the more you know, the less you know. In middle age I reserve my reverence for gardening experts. I listen to what they have to say more attentively than I do to news anchormen who talk and talk and don't give me any control over my little queendom. Priests give vague advice on how to be good, but there is nothing vague about what gardening experts will tell you. I approach them with awe.

"Do you need any help in the garden?" my neighbour asks.

"Why would I need help? I'm not working, I'm playing."

The man turns to his pretty wife and says: "At *her* age, it's play; at *our* age, it's work."

If you're young, you go to work, and if you're old, you go to the garden and have the time of your life. But then who is to say what is work, and what is play? The universe was made on the cheap. God volunteered his services.

The couple go on their merry way, and I decide to stop playing with fire, meaning I stop planting annuals and start pruning my lilac branches. Pruning them I feel as delighted as a six-year-old cutting up paper dresses for her paper dolls. I am happy, happier actually, than if I had won an all-expense paid trip to the Botanical Gardens in Paris. My backyard is my everyday City of Lights.

Wouldn't you know it—it starts to snow. (The weathergirl was right.) Do I take cover? I am too happy to be sensible. In fact, I am happy and naughty, or happy because I am a naughty; like a little girl splashing in a pool of water and getting her party dress dirtied, I am making a mess of things, and loving it. It sounds truly childish to admit to it, though at my age what is childish might smack of dementia …

I imagine those sitting on the bus, going to work in their office towers, looking at me gardening and envying me.

The phone rings.

"What did you do all day?" a friend asks.

"I spent the morning shopping for flowers and the afternoon planting them."

"She's an expert at doing nothing," I overhear her telling her sister who is listening in to the conversation.

So interior designers who are paid good money to jazz up a room are good citizens, and those who volunteer their talents, are bums, I wonder? Do-gooders aim to make the world a better place, as do gardeners, except gardeners succeed, and do-gooders often fail, I decide. Flower power is Divine power at its very best.

Rage = garbage. Flowers = white gold. I return and play hide and seek with my floral darlings in the front yard. And I am happy. Or almost happy. At least sex is not on my mind. Actually that's not true. Sex is on my mind; gardening helps keeps the frustration under control, but not all that much.

Like an illiterate longs to learn how to read and start her life all over again, be looked up to, I long to be re-educated with the warmth of a man's embrace, but it ain't going to happen. This old broad looks as sexually appetizing as a gorilla. There are sanctuaries for old gorillas, but what do you do with horny old females? In the days of yore my late husband came to my rescue. He was my Zoo Keeper and my Wizard of Oz. And now he's nowhere to be found. I can't find a silver lining in all this.

The snow turns to rain. I attack the blackberry bushes. Pruning the lilac bushes was a cinch compared to this. Watch out. A blackberry bush can cut through your skin, dead or alive. And that sets me thinking: Those who hurt you when they were alive can still hurt you after they are dead. (Take precautions.)

The wind picks up. It breaks my patio table apart, but not a single tulip is bent. Lesson here? It's possible to be strong and gentle (for sure).

"Aren't you cold?" a woman walking her dog asks.

"Oh no," I tell her, my hands as cold as ice.

"What a pretty garden you have," the woman says. The way I smile and say, "Thank you," you'd think I was some VIP waiting in line to get her honorary doctorate or something. Calling Dr. Mary ... The mother of all lessons: what you are looking for can be found right in your own backyard. (Or front yard.)

All very well, the compliments about my garden cheer me up, but not that much. My body is drying up and longs to be made wet. My late husband used to do it, and now he's not here. I miss him like a brook misses water if there were a drought. Wrong. A brook doesn't do any missing and my body actively misses my partner. I have the needs of a young woman and I am stuck in an old body. Sex appeal does not increase with age. If only our bodies were more like reversible rain jackets; as soon as one side is worn out, you could show off the other side. On my wish list: a reversible body beautiful.

That voice in my head says: "Turn to the mirror as you would to a friend who has betrayed you and you'll cry your heart out; turn to it as a friend who seeks to make amends, and you'll be ready to take on the day."

I can't imagine looking into a mirror and ever liking what I see, and yet, oddly enough, my body longs for a man's admiring glance like an actor longs for an audience! My late husband counted for many rows in a big auditorium. And now he's not there. My body longs for that old guy like a young bride waiting in church longs for the groom when he is half an hour late—what if he is not coming? My husband is definitely not coming and still my body longs for him. My life was so much better when my body was loved by him.

I never thought of a cunt as being particularly attractive but my late husband did. Like an ugly Pollock painting that sells for millions of dollars, my husband, the buyer, treated it with respect. And handled it with care.

In the army they teach recruits to accept the things they can't control and this helps reduce anxiety. Possibly if I thought of my garden as a boot camp (*ain't* no school), it might toughen me up.

The problem is I can't do the required exercises. I'm too old for anything and everything.

That in-the-skull therapist has an opinion: "Getting old poses danger. So you should think like a cat. Or a snake. Animals don't fret about their age—they seize the day. You can either give yourself up to your dead husband as a nun gives herself up to God, or if your body is reminding you that you are a beast at heart, act accordingly. Find yourself a mate."

How can I do that, I wonder?

The phone rings and this time it is my mother. She immediately and enthusiastically tells me that her neighbour's son—the one who went through a difficult divorce and custody battle a few years ago—is getting re-married. He lived alone for eight years and almost gave up hope of finding someone, but now at the age of 58, he is very much in love. I gather what she is trying to tell me is that if her neighbour has a second chance at love, so do I. Stories of Romeos and Juliets, under-aged, star-crossed lovers who outwit their parents, feed the spirit, as do those stories of over-the-hillers who beat the odds and fall in love. Believing happily-ever-after is possible at any age, in any country, in any shape or form, feels so very good. If a blind man can climb Mount Everest (it has been done), perhaps a not-so-young-lady like myself can climb atop a man's body and take pleasure.

A woman can't reverse the aging process, but she can change her attitude towards it—self-renewal on the cheap.

The weather turns really nasty. I decide I better take in the annuals I planted. Climbing the porch stairs, with a big pot of begonias, I don't know if I can master the art of aging, but as long as my legs hold out, I can still be of use.

Flowers are such impractical beauties; and yet, I am surprisingly in need of their company.

# 42

Dating—it's kind of like going to the circus, expecting to be entertained, and then, unexpectedly being asked to be part of the entertainment. Those who volunteer to go through a flaming ring of fire might, just might, get the surprise of their lives (love). There is no guarantee they will, but those who don't muster up the courage to participate don't have a chance in hell at it.

"Just do it," Olga says.

Over fifty falling in love is as difficult as swimming the length of Lake Ontario.

"It can be done."

"Not by me."

"Don't say that," Olga says. There is no pleasure in looking for a mate as there is no pleasure in being hungry. Hunger pangs can easily be satisfied, but those pangs related to love require super human will & strength. (No easy fixes.)

The idea of meeting someone from an on-line dating site is starting to be as repulsive as eating raw meat. (All sorts of bacteria like E. coli lurk there.)

"Don't worry; be happy," my friend says, picking the men I will agree to sit and chat with at a near-by café.

Going on a "coffee interview" is like going on an audition for a film called, "This Is Your Life." The casting director will decide whether or not you are right for the part. His decision is "Not" personal. Actors manage to learn to handle rejection, so can those who imagine themselves gifted in the art of loving. If only my late husband would step down from his heavenly throne and announce to the world that I am worthy of the lead part, but this is not about to happen.

Action ...

The twice-divorced man, an Italian, my age, is blessed with a teenage daughter, makes his own wine and loves to cook. He delivers pizza for a living, and while this in itself does not throw me off, the fact that he calls me "honey" does. He hints he is a good lover, and this is reason enough in his mind to have a real date. Dinner & dancing.

I say: "No."

"You could be the love of my life," he says.

I say: "No."

Two days pass. Another café. Another "coffee interview." This time the man I came across on the internet highway enters the pre-arranged public space on the arm of his grandson, a boy of ten.

"How old are you?" I ask the boy's grandpa.

"I have no age," he says.

His grandson whispers: "He's eighty-four." But the old man insists he has no age.

He has no large intestine either, but he is young at heart, and he loves to travel. Would I consider sharing accommodations with him on a cruise ship? I would, of course, be expected to pay for my own expenses.

I can't imagine myself undressing in front of this gentleman, let alone sharing his bed.

The next man I share a cup of coffee with is a financial planner whose leather jacket gives him a youthful air. His arrogance, intellectual pretensions, and right wing politics irritate me, but not half as much as his rude remarks concerning women of a certain age.

The sixty-two-year-old tells me: "Some women just want sex. I used to be OK with that, but now, I say, No."

The Aging Stud would like me as a client, but as for a love interest, well, I am the right height, but my boobs are the wrong size.

SOS. My late husband never did or said a thing to disparage my looks and now here I am at a café with a man who thinks he is a superhero; his 62-year-old cock has magic powers but it has a select clientele.

I would like to tell this fellow that I would rather see him lie in a pool of his own blood than see him naked on satin sheets, but I keep my mouth shut. His over-confidence repels me, as does his 62-year-old pot belly.

My late husband was a natural barrier between all those who would hurt me. He protected me like the ozone layer protects the earth from the ultraviolet rays of the sun.

He's not here now and I'm vulnerable. I feel exposed like an old drunk, half naked, sleeping on the sidewalk. I was addicted to his love. (The drink that made it possible for me Not to be an old drunk.) Now I am having withdrawal symptoms and I don't care if I freeze to death.

What would the late Dr. George Nemeth say to all this? Would he say something like "dreams rejuvenate the spirit; cynicism ages it?" Or would he recite the AA motto: "Accept the things you cannot change, and change the things you can?" I want his advice, but the doctor is not in. In days of old, in the film "This Is Your Life," my dear old husband (and sometime therapist) insisted I be given the lead roles, the choice parts, but nowadays he's not here and I have to audition for minor roles. There is no chance in hell I might get through the first round.

Action …

The next man I meet on-line is quite a-typical—tall, dark and handsome. (For real!) And better yet, he has a pleasant demure. The 68-year-old retired electrical engineer, a widower, misses his late wife and would have her back in a heartbeat but that's out of the question, and so here he is. He can manage on his own, but he would rather not. He is looking for a serious relationship, a life partner.

The first hour, and then to the second, and by the third, the man thinks he and I are ready to spend the week-end together.

"Who wouldn't like you?" he says.

Who wouldn't like him, I think to myself. He's well-mannered, well-educated and well-spoken; he's smart and sweet, and he's sexy. He's decent. He's civil. And he's kind-hearted. If I were in an elevator, during a blackout, this is the man I would want to find myself with. I feel safe with him. And yet here I am at a café, and I am longing to get out. It's not him I want, but my late husband.

"Can I call you?" the widower asks.

I hesitate.

Spring Moon

# WHAT IS IMPOSSIBLE FOR MEN
# IS POSSIBLE FOR GOD
## (Luke 18:27)

Year Ten

# 43

Medicine for the soul: promises. The best is yet to come. Driven by an animal desire to mate, to be part of a unit, two in one, believing pleasure is possible at any age, wanting Not to be alone (a basic instinct), desiring romance, companionship and the freedom to be myself (flawed & all), I agree to yet another coffee interview with yet another man I come across on the internet dating highway. I expect another exercise in polite conversation, another trip to the dark side, another rejection. (One of us will undoubtedly say no and what if I am the one told: "No, No, absolutely not?")

The moment I see him I know he is the man for me. How I know it, I am not sure; all I do know is that I like the look of him. I like his East European accent. (How can I not, considering I was married to someone who had the same vocal proclivities?) I find myself at ease; I like chatting with this 66-year-old unpretentious and affable fellow. It's the first time I meet a stranger that I was matched with by a machine when I don't want to run away, rush out the door, and look for my late husband. I want to stay right where I am and listen to the details of his life story. After an hour, I want another. And then another.

Like wanting to eat, wanting water (no explanation needed), like wanting to read the morning newspaper or wanting to travel and see the world, I want the pleasure of this man's company. There is no madness driving this want. Like wanting peace over war, like wanting an end to child slavery, child hunger and child abuse, or like wanting a cure for cancer, my desire to pair up and attach myself to this individual makes sense. He offers solace. Warmth. Oddly (or not so oddly) he is a loner, like I am.

"When can I see you again?" he asks before I leave. The next day the same question is asked. And the next. By the end of the first week, it's set in stone—we're a couple. By the end of the first month, it's understood we'll live together, and become common-law partners.

I hadn't thought it possible I could ever enjoy and be relaxed in the company of someone other than my late husband, but here I am conversing, untroubled by my mad impulses to dislike myself. In his company I have the sense of having won a major victory against myself. My self-doubts and anxieties do not defeat me. I manage to employ common sense and allow my higher self (my more loving self) to reign. In his company I get a glimpse of what my life was like, and what it could be like again—a life shared with a significant other. And it's wonderful!

I have the sensation I am travelling back in time to when I was a young woman, waiting for a slew of good things to happen. (And they did happen!) I yearn for this man's company like I yearn for the sun to show up after days of rain. It's that simple a thing.

Like a cat in heat yearns to do what nature intended—I yearn to be his. Admittedly there is something animalistic about this yearning, but there is also a spiritual quality to it. A holiness. Like a Catholic nun yearns for Holy Communion, I yearn for his kiss. Copulation is a predetermined animal act, predetermined for procreation and yet even if you are no longer in the procreation mode (eggless) you are still capable of a kiss. No one is ever too old for pleasure.

Second chances don't come often, but when they do, it feels as if angels were dancing on the head of a pin—just for you. Love is the antidote to loneliness.

Like a carpenter who after years of making kitchen cabinets has been commissioned to carve statues of Jesus and make art, I take pride in having been given the chance to change directions. You might think it rather blasphemous to bring Jesus into this conversation, but then, wasn't it Jesus who saved Mary Magdalene from being stoned to death by declaring we're all sinners? All of us sin against the dead by forgetting them. We forget those we loved and have passed away like we forget our elementary school teachers; they were nice enough when we were young, but now that we have incorporated what they taught, they're erased.

That in-the-skull therapist has an opinion: "Happiness is a choice. Either you will to live and live well, or you stagnate and are miserable. There is no art to loving or to making love (an effortless A plus is guaranteed). It's an exercise of will—the will to courage, the will to be yourself, whatever the risk."

# 44

I can imagine a world without politicians and am OK with it, but a world without well-fed babies laughing, and doing nothing in life but wanting to be fed and enjoyed, is not a world I would want to be a part of. Blossoms add colour and fragrance; so do babies. They do more than mask the stench of sadness—they eliminate it.

A baby shower is in the works and my cousin—the grandmother-to-be—is all smiles. Studying the fruit tree blossoms in her garden, I feel like a child on her first day at school, as well as that same child all grown up, enjoying an extended summer vacation from college. A second sniff of the said blossoms (apple or pear?) and I am certain when I die I will go to heaven. (There is a heaven to go to.) Apple blossoms advertise God exists and He's everyone's Great Grandpa.

The young mother-to-be being celebrated strolls down the garden path like an Academy Award winner. She is living proof that it is still possible to create a thing of beauty—glorious and sacrosanct.

One comes into this world attached to another. Even those infants who are abandoned at birth gain entry into this sacred abode called Earth tied to another. Possibly, newborns are dying to tell those who take them in: "God is in me. You have no choice—you must love me."

Life renews itself—grass, trees, even babies renew themselves. (They get a full load of new skin every month.) Renewal is coded into our DNA. That's why men and women gravitate towards each other—in their mating the promise of rebirth. Progress ...

On the table: loads of home-baked goods. My mother's—the most prized of them all.

A friend of a friend, an out-of-towner, after complimenting my mother on her out-of-this-world, rich-tasting almond biscotti, turns to me and says: "How was it that you found someone on a dating site the very first month you joined? I have been on a couple of sites for years and not found anyone."

"It's possible my late husband had a hand in helping me find someone—I had an advantage."

"Highly unlikely," she says.

"But not impossible."

And that sets me thinking ... I have a new partner and he makes me happy but I still miss my late husband. I thought I could only miss him if I were sad, but I was wrong. Before, without a partner, I missed him as one misses being healthy when one is sick, but now I am not sick, and I am still missing him. I miss the familiarity of being with my husband as one misses one's home when one is travelling. Home sweet home: my husband.

"Is your new partner anything like your old one?" the out-of-towner, a divorcee, asks.

"Both were refugees from Communist countries," I tell her. "Sometimes I find myself unable to tell the new man in my life from the old one, and not because they're similar (they're not), but because they both serve the same function. (Caring for me!)"

I mix the two up like I mix up socks. That may sound downright trite, but that's how it is—they're both essential to my somewhat dull & ordinary existence. Or maybe I should put it another way—I mix them up, like I mix up Bach and Mozart. Experts know who wrote what, but I can't tell their music apart—both are divine in my book. Or, it's not that I can't tell one man from the other, but rather that they're part of the same whole—like a sweater made with two different colours of wool, the mixture creates a beautiful design. Supposedly love is blind, but what if it is more of an eye patch—a medicinal aid?

"You don't know how lucky you are," the out-of-towner says.

"I suppose," I say.

"Anything missing?"

"A grandchild."

To my mind babies are vital to a life well-lived but that's neither here nor there, as I have no say in the matter. It's out of my control.

What to do?

a) Turn to the mirror and write three wishes on it;

b) Turn to the mirror as if it were a kitten you were considering to adopt and be comforted by or,

c) Turn to the mirror as if it were a burning bush, and you, Moses. (Anything is possible.)

The out-of-towner dismisses my wish for a grandchild, and says: "Personally, if I had to do it all over again, I would not have any children. They're a pain in the neck."

The out-of-towner hurries off to talk to another guest, and I walk towards my own mother, wondering if she has ever wished I had not entered her life. When I was a teenager she and I had many an argument.

That voice in my head tells me: "You must forgive those who hurt you. (That's an order!) You must be friendly. Everyone comes out of the same womb (God's) and everyone will return to the same household (God's). Whether your aging parents or your adult children love you is of little consequence, because when it comes to love, you could be the one delivering the goods—good will, good intentions and good cheer. Commit an act of kindness and you become wholly one with God—everyman's Dr. Feel Good."

That voice in my head can't belong to the late Dr. Nemeth— that man did not pin his hopes on God helping anybody. (That's why down-to-earth therapists were needed.) Could it be he has changed his tune? Months ago I had a dream in which I heard him say: "Mary, what is ..." I had assumed he wanted to ask me a question, but what if he simply had wanted to say: "What is impossible for man, is possible for God (Luke 18:27)?"

I'll never know what my late husband was trying to say that day. All I can be sure of is this: when you are loved all is well with the world. Whether it is one person loving you, or a dozen, or even if you are alone loving yourself, you are good enough as is! Call it wishful thinking, or call it the miracle of self-deception, whatever it is, it works wonders.

# 45

At daybreak I head for the office: my backyard. The more flowers, the fatter my pay cheque: happiness. True wealth. Every flower is a living I.O.U.

Thought of the day: I would rather stroll down a garden path, than climb the slippery staircase to heaven. The mother of all lessons: Stay in the moment. An old cliché, but one worth repeating.

Like stars of Broadway shows, gardeners are presented with bouquets of flowers for a job well done. The words "a job well done" are music to one's ears; the words "thank you," a short prayer.

Every flower is an alarm clock. It wakes you up and tells you: "I do like you. I do like you!" In every flower: hope.

In my backyard I want for nothing. Actually, I am freed of wanting: a blessed state. In my backyard I am in The No Nonsense Church of Mercy. I love one and all. Looking after flowers, making the world a prettier place, is a good deed that doesn't go unnoticed. Assist the Head Gardener with his duties, and that could be your ticket to heaven. Pretty flowers, pretty thoughts: bouquets of grace.

I take the shovel and dig into the rocky soil—triumph. Like an astronaut who has landed on the moon and placed the flag of her beloved country into the rocky ground, I came, saw and colonized.

Gardening in my high heels, I feel like a child bride. My groom: the sun. It warms me up with thoughts of summer fragrances. And afternoon delights.

Time to be happy. Be a child at play. The sun doesn't act his age (forever playing ball), nor does God. Lesson here—Don't act your age, and you might live forever????

"If you know the answer, why ask?" someone suggests. (Who?)

Aging is a form of forced migration; you move from one year to the next. Like moving from one country to another, the scenery changes, as do the people and the climate. At times you get nostalgic for the old country (youth), and at other times you feel so much at home where you are that the idea of returning to the place you began is repugnant. In the fall birds migrate to warmer climates; their flight plan is pre-determined—but what they carry in their beaks (seeds) can fall anywhere. Possibly God has us in his beak and when we fall out of it life blossoms?????

Perhaps I should stop asking questions about the Almighty Enigma, and start writing odes to Mother Nature ... "Spring (a mute) is a philosopher unable to offer words—only highfalutin thoughts. Rediscover its 'Arguments on Being' and you will close all books. This particular philosopher king knows how to run a true workers' state. (Manifesto # 1: Flowers are good weapons against the class system.) Nothing is askew on a planet which allows the dictum of this mute to override Plato's or Marx's. Theologians, politicians, office clerks, wordy university students, and talk therapists should take heed. Spring is retraining its flowery staff to say nothing. (No swearing, please!) The mute will surrender its extravaganza of good ideas and everyone with a head on their shoulders will surrender all of their bad ones."

Is artistic creation a worthy pursuit? Nature makes flowers and what do artists do? They make stuff. Spent flowers can help fertilize next year's crop, but what happens to those paintings and books and sculptures folk get tired of? Now that's a sad thought, and I was all set to cheer myself up.

The fact is nature recycles. (Spent sperm is turned into a baby!) Possibly our creative drive, our spirits—our very souls—are also of value. That's why they're not terminated. There is no death?????

I look at a flower with one purpose in mind. The Beatific Vision ought to stare at me. Does it now?

Possibly God is too busy directing the sun, the key player in his celestial show of force, to put himself on display. The sun has been doing the same vaudeville routine for years, yet the act still feels fresh. That voice in my head (is it the late Dr. Nemeth?) says: "Set your alarm clock for the greatest show on earth and you won't be disappointed."

Thought of the day: Use a daisy to look at God. Keep off the grass.

Another thought: Turn to the mirror as if it were a window—the reflection on it isn't half as interesting as what lies beyond it.

I need God's mercy as plants need rain. If mercy is dispensed as is rain, I could get lucky, but if it's given out as are coins from a slot machine, I'm in trouble.

Spring is in full swing, delivering good tidings and good cheer. In the spring I hover over my garden like an angel missing a wing, meaning I manage quite well despite my shortcomings. In the spring I am self-sufficient. My garden lifts me up just high enough for me to see how beautiful my life is.

I can turn to the mirror as if it were a murderer on the loose, and I, its next victim. Or I can turn away from the mirror and admire a morning glory.

Because God made the flowers, maybe, just maybe God made me, and well then, if both the flowers and I have the same Creator, then there must be something of the flowers in me—something beautiful. It doesn't matter if I'm fifty years old or sixty years old; all my sad dark thoughts have to fall to the ground and make room for something new. Or better yet, they can be recycled—used to make wisdom (spirit mulch). I must take pride in all of God's creations, including in what goes by my name.

That voice in my head voices approval: "That's it. Each bouquet of flowers is a mirror. Look and be amazed. What is happiness? What is joy? Can money buy happiness? Yes, it can, but if it's The Good Life you are after, joy is it and it's not for sale. Joy is not aligned to your net worth, education level, or country of origin. Unlike grace, it's not a gift randomly distributed by God. To get joy you have to change how you think. You have to follow Moses' Ten Commandments (a do-gooders' self-help guide) and uphold the Hippocratic Oath. (Do no harm!) You also have to trade in self-hate for self-acceptance. That's hard work. Can you do it?"

I can't do it. SOS.

Calling the late Dr. George Nemeth. What does he have to say to all this? If he had one last word, what would he say?

"Be kind to yourself."

Is that it—be kind to yourself?

That voice in my head insists: "Time is not a renewable resource. You can worry about the moment of impact (dying) or you can take solace in the fact that you are presently in good health. Love your backyard. Love your cat. Love whomever dares to love you, and dared to love you. The dead still have power. Love them and they will love you in return."

But what happens, I wonder, when there is no love to be found? Then what?

My in-house therapist has an answer (he always does): "I dare you to love yourself. (Love yourself!) I dare you to dream. Be young at heart. Have a sense of humour. I dare you to discover it is possible to enjoy the mundane. Even failure can be savoured. Failure stops you from looking down on others, and it reinforces what you already know: you don't have to be a success to be loved. Failure strengthens the will to humility. Be humble, and compassion sets in. Besides, revisions can be made to any story, including your own. Change what you don't like. Act. Cherish the moment. I dare you to believe God is your friend. I dare you to be yourself (be stripped of artifice). Dare me to love you and I will. Turn to the mirror and say: 'I love you world, please love me too.'"

Everyone knows it—dreams rejuvenate the spirit, cynicism ages it. Everyone knows it—children can cheer you up. Music can cheer you up. And so can a garden. Walk into a garden and you will feel rescued.

Plants live in silence and they don't judge those who admire them. Plants are the most unselfish creatures, giving up their vitamins and minerals without a word of complaint; plants don't chide us when we cut them down; they don't express grief or anger or talk back at us. Plants' silent breath sweetens the air. Plants know all about the joy of giving, and the joy of giving is a quiet pleasure.

I can imagine a world without books, but I can't imagine one without flowers. Books make promises; flowers deliver on them.

Every flower is a holy picture. An image of the Divine. Instant faith.

Every flower is a love letter. The question is: Who sent it? Was it God? Return to sender? Can't do so. Address unknown.

Who knows what God is? All you can be certain of is that God is old. A *Guinness World Book Record* holder.

You can learn as much from a book as from a flower. A book (let's say Tolstoy's *War and Peace*) takes time and patience, but a flower gives its reader everything away in a flash.

Books inspire revolutions; flowers, gratitude.

Every flower is an instant bestseller. Shakespeare-in-the-making. Every garden contains an entire library of classics.

Any pot full of flowers, strategically placed in your front yard (a floral focal point) is a welcome sign. Come on in.

In my dreams I am a little girl who can flap her arms and head straight to heaven. In reality my wings are clipped.

Someone suggests (my therapist?): "You can't love flowers and not be an angel at heart."

Thought of the day: Give me flowers, or give me miracles.

# About the Author

MARY MELFI was born in Italy. In 1957, at the age of six, she immigrated with her family to Montreal, Quebec where she attended the local English schools. She received a B.A. from Concordia University and a Masters from McGill University. After completing her studies, she married Dr. George Nemeth, had two children, and published over a dozen books of critically-acclaimed poetry, prose and plays. Her first novel, *Infertility Rites* (Guernica Editions, 1991) was translated into French and Italian. Her memoir, *Italy Revisited* (Guernica Editions, 2009), which offers an intimate look at the day-to-day social, cultural, religious and work activities of those living in the Italian countryside prior to World War II, was also translated into both French and Italian. The French version was translated by Claude Bèland; it was published under the title *Là bas, en Italie* (Editions Triptyque, 2015). Also a playwright, Melfi's comedy, *My Italian Wife*, was produced by the Sons of Italy in 2015. Her most recent publication, a novel, *Via Roma* (Guernica Editions, 2015) is set to be published in French. Adapted by the author for the stage, *Via Roma* has been described as a "murder mystery with a romantic and metaphysical twist." Mary Melfi received the *Giornata Internazionale Della Donna* Award in 2010. More information is available on the author's website: www.italyrevisited.org.

# Praise for the Author's Works

Melfi ... thrives as a powerful force in the Canadian literary landscape, exposing readers to images, ideas and conceptions of reality we could otherwise never have imagined.
—*Italian Canadiana (Vol. XXX, 2016)*

Mary Melfi has a broad range. Throughout her decades as a writer, she has explored issues of identity, relationships and 'internalized psychological conflicts' in her works of prose, theatre and fiction ... Her writing is humorous and truthful."
—*Panoram Italia (June/July 2015)*

Selon moi, elle est un des plus grands écrivains de ce pays.
—*Antonio D'Alfonso (préface/ Là-bas, en Italie: Editions Triptyque, 2015)*

Her writings are characterized by an avant-garde sensibility that transgresses the conventions of a given literary form (whether it is poetry, drama or fiction). In each of works poetry verges on prose, fiction is penetrated by poetic and dramatic devices, and a play has poetic and narrative elements – though the distinctiveness of the given form is not erased. Ideas about identity and

culture that flow out of English-Canadian and Italian-Canadian/Québécois experiences interpenetrate each other. Melfi is interested in the metaphysical side of human existence, the difficulties of establishing a coherent feminine identity, cultural dislocation, and the artist's attempt to create a new reality.
— *The Oxford Companion to Canadian Literature (1997)*


(*Via Roma*, Guernica Editions, 2015) The underlying themes of sex, death and dreams—all Freudian concerns—are skillfully explored in this novel … Despite its serious subject matter, *Via Roma: Between 2 Worlds, 2 Men* is fun to read. The voice is original, the novel full of witty one-liners and quirky insights.
— *The Ottawa Review of Books (December 2015)*


(*Via Roma*, Guernica Editions, 2015) Mary Melfi … is no doubt part of the multicultural canon in Canada, or at the very least has a secure niche in Italo-Canadian letters. *Via Roma* is a novel driven by the main character Sophie Wolfe and sets out to be philosophically wise, witty, and alternating between lustful lament, celebration, and tragic undertow, and finally a meditation on life versus the after-life … It is a tragic-comic novel full of the ups and downs, torments and pleasures of love found and lost, and found again in the birth of a child.
— *The Winnipeg Review (September 2016)*


(*Italy Revisited*, Guernica Editions, 2009) In a unique approach to memoirs, Mary Melfi writes her autobiography as a double memoir in a conversation between herself and her mother. In the process, readers become eye witnesses to life in a southern Italian village at the turn of the 20th century. The narrative also explores the complexities of mother-daughter relationships, especially those found in immigrant families.
— *Italian America (Winter 2010)*

(*Italy Revisited*, Guernica Editions, 2009) Mary Melfi explores a mother-daughter dialogue that gives life to the mother's memories of mid-century southern Italy while also revealing truths about relationships that sometimes exist between immigrant mothers and their children."
— *Concordia University Magazine (Spring 2010)*


(*Là-bas, en Italie*, les Editions Triptyque, 2015) Je commence avec quelque chose d'absolument délicieux, *Là-bas, en Italie* de Marie Melfi. J'ai tellement aimé ce livre, je l'ai lue le plus lentement possible, en même temps, c'est comme un sac de chips, tu ne peux pas t'en arrêter … C'est chaleureux, c'est charmant, c'est réjouissant, c'est émouvant, c'est un bonheur de début jusqu'à la fin, j'ai adoré ça. C'est remarquablement écrit. Je ne connaissais pas cet auteur, elle a fait d'autres choses et j'ai hâte de la découvrir. Un cadeau!
— *Chrystine Brouillet, TVA Salut, Bonjour Weekend (January 23, 2016)*


(*Là-bas, en Italie*, les Editions Triptyque, 2015) L'écriture est simple, naturelle, sans prétention, le récit est empreint de tendresse et, en prime, on apprend un tas de choses sur l'Italie, là-bas.
— *Lettres québécoises, la revue de l'actualité littéraire (Été, 2016)*


(*Foreplay and My Italian Wife*, Guernica Editions, 2012) Both *Foreplay* and *My Italian Wife* examine the complex dynamics in any relationship—love, trust, and sex. *Foreplay* centers around the relationship of an emotionally insecure couple that take a much-needed vacation on a New Age remote island in order to improve their sex lives. The more light-hearted tongue-in-cheek *My Italian Wife* looks at the mind-set and preoccupations of second-generation Italian immigrants.
— *Italocanadese (October 2012)*

(*Office Politics*, Guernica Editions, 1999) In *Office Politics*, Melfi tackles the modern workplace. Her poems are about how the powerful manipulate the powerless. There are keen observations about the anxieties, tensions and frustrations of those who have to satisfy the whims of bosses ...
— *The Suburban (March 2000)*


(*Stages: Selected Poems*, Guernica Editions, 1998) Like a surrealist painter, Melfi produces fantastic and dreamlike images ... Melfi's landscape touches the unconscious, and takes the reader to a different reality.
— *The Canadian Book Review Annual (2000)*


(*Painting Moments: Art, AIDS and Nick Palazzo*, Guernica, 1998) Pays homage to a tragically brief life with excerpts from Palazzo's journals, the reminiscences of friends, short essays, his art and mostly full-page, colour reproductions of 18 of his powerful pieces.
— *The Toronto Star (October 3, 1998)*


(*Sex Therapy*, a black comedy, Guernica Editions, 1996) *Sex Therapy*, like other work by Mary Melfi, brings together a variety of elements: the anxieties of modern womanhood; and the textures and feelings of living in Italian and Canadian culture. These elements are shot through with Melfi's wit, bouts of black humour. In her own way, she celebrates the absurdities of contemporary human existence.
—*AICW Bollettino (Winter 1996)*


(*Ubu, the Witch Who Would be Rich*, Doubleday Canada, 1994) An imaginative, funny story, Ubu gives us a futuristic world of good witches, bad witches, high tech and hilarious stock characters.
—*McGill News (Summer 1994)*

(*Ubu, the Witch Who Would be Rich*, Doubleday Canada, 1994) This is a witch tale unlike any you've come across ... Readers aged 13 and up may find this bewitching.
— *The Toronto Star (April 24, 1994)*


(*Infertility Rites*, Guernica Editions, 1991) A bitterly funny first novel ... Melfi has taken on a tough and important issue for women and, for the most part, handles it with flair ... The adorably whiny and angst-ridden Nina is a wonderful creation.
— *The Toronto Globe and Mail (Sept. 21, 1991)*


(*Infertility Rites*) Melfi is an able writer. Her prose draws one into the story and holds the reader's attention until the end of the book. Her allusions and conceits are ironic and clever.
— *Canadian Book Review Annual (1992)*


(*A Dialogue with Masks*, Mosaic Press, 1985) Sex, death and power are the explicit themes, but a persistent and irreconcilable disparity in their views underlies the exchange. John Fowles' *Mantissa* was a similar experiment in the contest between the sexes, but where Fowles' book brought unexpected transformations and humour to the subject, Melfi brings an intermittent poet's sensitivity to the language of dispute ...
— *The Toronto Globe & Mail (June 21, 1986)*


(*A Season in Beware*, Black Moss Press, 1989) In places this book is breath-taking. If Sylvia Plath had lived, perhaps she'd write like this.
— *Next Exit (April 1990)*

(*A Season in Beware*, Black Moss Press, 1989) In the last decade, Mary Melfi has published several works of poetry and fiction and with *A Season in Beware* she continues to emerge as one of this country's finest poets.
—*Italian Canadiana (Vol. 9, 1993)*


(*A Bride in Three Acts*, poetry, Guernica Editions, 1983) When people in the twenty-first century want an indication of what it was like to be a woman in the 1980s, they can read *A Bride in Three Acts*, Mary Melfi's third book of poetry ... In her oblique, often whimsical style, she postulates the myths, the hoaxes, the ennui women must live with and the repercussions of these on the female psyche.
—*Room of One's Own (August 1984)*


(*A Queen is Holding a Mummified Cat*, Guernica Editions, 1982) Takes the reader on an intriguing and sometimes terrifying journey ... Unforgettable surrealism.
—*Mamashee (Summer 1982)*


(*A Queen is Holding a Mummified Cat*, Guernica Editions, 1982) A young and brilliant Italo-Canadian poet.
—*Contemporary Verse II (May 1984)*